NO
ESCAPE

NO ESCAPE

THE MEMOIRS OF A POW IN

STALAG XXA

VIC MARKHAM

Pen & Sword
MILITARY

AN IMPRINT OF PEN & SWORD BOOKS LTD.
YORKSHIRE - PHILADELPHIA

First published in Great Britain in 2025 by
PEN AND SWORD MILITARY
An imprint of
Pen & Sword Books Limited
Yorkshire – Philadelphia

Copyright © Michael Markham, 2025

ISBN 978 1 03612 124 2

The right of Michael Markham to be identified as Author of this work has been asserted by him in accordance with the Copyright, Designs and Patents Act 1988.

A CIP catalogue record for this book is available from the British Library.

All rights reserved. No part of this book may be reproduced, transmitted, downloaded, decompiled or reverse engineered in any form or by any means, electronic or mechanical including photocopying, recording or by any information storage and retrieval system, without permission from the Publisher in writing. NO AI TRAINING: Without in any way limiting the Author's and Publisher's exclusive rights under copyright, any use of this publication to "train" generative artificial intelligence (AI) technologies to generate text is expressly prohibited. The Author and Publisher reserve all rights to license uses of this work for generative AI training and development of machine learning language models.

Typeset in Times New Roman 11/14.5 by
SJmagic DESIGN SERVICES, India.
Printed and bound in the UK by CPI Group (UK) Ltd.

The Publisher's authorised representative in the EU for product safety is Authorised Rep Compliance Ltd., Ground Floor, 71 Lower Baggot Street, Dublin D02 P593, Ireland.
www.arccompliance.com

For a complete list of Pen & Sword titles please contact
PEN & SWORD BOOKS LIMITED
George House, Units 12 & 13, Beevor Street, Off Pontefract Road, Barnsley, South Yorkshire, S71 1HN, England
E-mail: enquiries@pen-and-sword.co.uk
Website: www.pen-and-sword.co.uk

or

PEN AND SWORD BOOKS
1950 Lawrence Rd, Havertown, PA 19083, USA
E-mail: uspen-and-sword@casematepublishers.com
Website: www.penandswordbooks.com

CONTENTS

Introduction		vii
Preface		viii
Phase One	The Second World War started for me in September 1938	1
Phase Two	I was ordered to report to Euston Station on 12 October 1939 to the Territorial Army	8
Phase Three	I was woken at 5 a.m. on 10 May 1940 by the sound of bombing	14
Phase Four	30 May 1940 – the Germans greeted us with 'Ah ha Tommy! For you the war is over, in three weeks we shall be in England'	28
Phase Five	July 1940 – Torn would be the HQ for Stalag XX-A	36
Phase Six	November 1940 – We were sent to Camp 13A	47
Phase Seven	February 1941 – I was taken out of this dreadful camp 13A and sent about a quarter of a mile up the road to Fort 13	55
Phase Eight	May 1941 – Fort 14 was the hospital	59

NO ESCAPE: THE MEMOIRS OF A POW IN STALAG XXA

Phase Nine	August 1943 – Fort 15 was a 'Non-arbeiters' camp	106
Phase Ten	November 1943 – back to Fort 14	110
Phase Eleven	August 1944 – we move to 'Kopernikus Lager'	118
Phase Twelve	January 1945 – the Red Army began to advance again	123
Phase Thirteen	11 April 1945 – being released	138
Phase Fourteen	22 April 1945 – after five years, a POW's view of the White Cliffs of Dover was overwhelming	143
Letters home		147

INTRODUCTION

All my working life, since the age of 14, has been spent in advertising, marketing and public relations.

I now work, part-time, as a tutor in Business Colleges in Oxford. I have had a very wide, practical experience, not only in the UK and Europe, but around the world. My students tell me that I am a great story teller who can bring my subjects to life. In the early 1970s I was asked to write two books on my specialist subjects and I found it easier to 'tell my story' to my secretary.

It was therefore appropriate that in telling my experiences during the Second World War that I told my story into a tape recorder.

The tapes have lain around for many years waiting for my grandchildren to grow old enough to be interested in hearing 'Grandad's story'.

I have now had the tapes transcribed so that not only my grandchildren but my friends can read the story. It is very much a spoken rather than a written narrative. It is of a different world, a different time, with quite different values to the 1990s.

PREFACE

This story of life in a German POW camp in the Second World War is different from the normal British POW story in a number of ways.

To start with I was a gunner in the Royal Artillery – not an officer – who was accepted by the German authorities as a medical orderly and, therefore, protected personnel.

Stalag XX-A in Thorn, West Prussia (now Torun in Poland) where I served the bulk of my – nearly – five years in captivity, was guarded by German soldiers of the Wehrmacht who were in an enemy country (and, with much hatred towards them, found life in the town very different), whereas we were in a friendly country (Britain started the war against Germany ostensibly to defend Poland) and we were treated with great friendship by the populace.

As a medical orderly in the Stalag Hospital (Fort 14) I was chosen, by the British doctors, to be a member of a group of twenty-five whose task it was to deal with a possible typhoid epidemic such as that suffered by British POWs in the First World War. The reason why only twenty-five were chosen from the staff of the hospital was because only enough Canadian anti-typhus serum was supplied by the Red Cross to treat that number.

Quite early on in POW life, the men working in the hospital and the rest of the Stalag were instructed by the Senior British Officer (SBO and a doctor) NOT to try to escape back to Britain. The reason for this command was because we were 'other ranks' and under the terms of the Geneva Convention 'other ranks' were expected to work – AND any British POW trying to escape would be helped by the Polish civilians. Any Pole found by

PREFACE

the Germans to have helped a British POW to escape was shot. The SBO decided that it was futile to lose the life of anyone just to let an 'other rank' try to escape. So firm orders were issued to that effect.

So our life in Fort 14, the Stalag XX-A hospital, was nothing like Colditz or Stalag Luft III. However, there can be no doubt at all that the members of the Stalag XX-A in general, and the staff of the hospital, in particular, were a great thorn in the side of the German authorities.

PHASE ONE

The Second World War started for me in September 1938, at about the time Chamberlain, the British prime minister, was going to Munich to meet Hitler. The country was in a state of hysteria and I really thought that war was going to start immediately. That the bombs were going to fall.

The key horror we were really concerned about, in those days, was gas – particularly mustard gas, which caused dreadful blisters. I cannot tell you what a hatred we had of gas.

We had all seen the pictures of the First World War with soldiers streaming back, blinded and gasping for breath and with awful sores. Not unlike those you see from Hiroshima and, therefore, we were as desperately scared about gas as people of today are of the nuclear bomb.

There was a tremendous outcry by ordinary people that they wanted gas masks issued and the government had to bow to their wishes with the result that in October, just after Munich, I, as a member of the 28th Willesden Scout Group, went down to Furness Road School to help get very frightened people into a queue to be fitted with gas masks.

Every single person in the country, man, woman and child (children had special gas masks) was fitted with a gas mask. All were trembling and tearful. That was my first introduction to the horrors of war.

In December 1938, the 28th Willesden Rover Scouts decided that what we would all join the Police War Reserve. By joining the police we could still continue with our scouting activities, whereas if we joined the Territorial Army we would have wasted our scouting skills and knowledge. So off we went to the police station in the Harrow Road to join the Police War Reserves.

NO ESCAPE: THE MEMOIRS OF A POW IN STALAG XXA

During the early part of 1939, we had regular meetings at the Harrow Road police station, receiving instruction, which was very detailed, on first aid, how to handle drunks, how to break into a house, how to pickpocket, or rather how to see pickpockets in action. We also went on patrol with the local policeman around Paddington. It was a very interesting and, I thought, a very worthwhile job to do.

However, the government had other plans.

In February 1939, the government, for the very first time in Britain's history, introduced conscription in peace time. Their plan was to call up 20-year-olds for six months, the object being to train them to be soldiers! They said six months is not very long but it will give you an introduction to soldiering.

At least that was the plan.

We were called the militia. I still have the booklet on its background and history on file; as I was 20 years of age, I was called up into the army.

In July 1939, I had to register for service and went to Harlesden for a medical. It was a joke. The doctors were not really interested or even serious about a medical exam. We were only going for six months' training and the doctors felt it would do us good. We all passed the medical and then we were handed over to the army who were in the same building. We were asked what unit we wanted to join. One thing for sure was that I did not want to go marching so I said, 'Can I go into the Royal Artillery?' And they said, 'OK.'

Now because the name Markham comes later in the alphabet I was due to be called up in October and not in August with the first batch. What I though most significant was that when I reported to the police that I was due to be called up in the militia I asked, 'Do you want me to continue in the police war reserve?' and they said, 'Oh yes please,' and I said, 'But I'm going to be called up in October,' and they said, 'Well don't worry about that. Would you please continue to service in the Police War Reserves until you join the militia.'

Later when I looked at my call-up papers for the Police War Reserve I saw that it was typed out and dated 27 March 1939, so there was no doubt about it that the police really wanted me to stay on until I was called up in the army.

The authorities really expected the German Air Force to bomb England (particularly London) heavily from Day One of the war and anticipated very heavy casualties, which the police would have had to control.

PHASE ONE

<u>So here it was in August 1939</u>, I was an active member of the Police War Reserve, and I had had my medical and my call-up papers to join the army in October.

In August, I went on my summer holiday to Germany as one of the members of an organisation call ITT – International Tramping Tours. It was an inexpensive way of getting around Europe. We were to go walking and it seemed very enjoyable. Jack Sweet, a great friend of mine, had been on a couple of these ventures with his wife and thought they were marvellous.

So I had written off to ITT and applied to go to the Black Forest. They wrote back and said, 'Mr Markham, there are twenty-four people on this party of which you are the only male and if you would like to withdraw we could transfer you to a trip to Austria with fifteen men and fifteen women.'

I changed tours.

On 12 August, I went to Liverpool Street station at the start of my holiday.

It was quite interesting really. In those days when you went abroad you really felt you were going abroad.

We left Liverpool Street station to go to Harwich to catch the overnight ferry crossing and then on to Antwerp. The next morning, the ship sailed down the River Scheldt. It was a fascinating trip. We were then off-loaded at the quayside where we joined a train to take us to Basle where we were going to link up with some Germans who were joining our group.

It was a combined men and women and combined English/German tour. Most of the other members of the party were from Peace Pledge Union and they thought it gave a balance to have somebody like me who was a militia man. We stayed overnight in Basle. Basle is in three parts, there is the Swiss Basle, the French Basle and the German Basle.

On Monday we went into Nazi Germany. Honestly, there was a terrible atmosphere the moment we walked into Germany, with black-uniformed, swastika-armbanded men at the station.

We got on the train and travelled by the side of Lake Constance past Friedrichshafen where the Zeppelins had been based in 1918. At the end of Lake Constance is a very nice little town called Bregenz where we stayed the night.

Franz, a German, who acted as our guide, suggested that we ought to go for a stroll to get our limbs loosened up after the two days in the train. The 'stroll' took us up a hill which is higher than Mount Snowdon! It was a really tough 'stroll', but it was marvellous with a wonderful view of the lake.

We spent a wonderful holiday in the mountains and at the end of the fortnight we journeyed to Innsbruck where there was tremendous tension. In the papers the next morning, 24 August 1939, there it was, sprawled all over the front page: Germany and Russia had signed a non-aggression pact. The war started on 31 August.

Germany was being mobilised for war, and we saw men in uniform saying goodbye to their families as they went off to war. Our German friend, Franz, was really fearful of the prospect of war. Also in our party was a young German woman called Adele. She was a full-blooded Nazi and Adele and I had argued the whole holiday. The British members of the group, apart from me, were members of the Peace Pledge Union and smuggled Franz over the border into Switzerland as a member of our party.

However, we really did not know the war was going to start as quickly as that. It took us two or three days to get back home. I arrived on Saturday, 26 August, rested on the Sunday and was back at work on the Monday morning. During that week, there were obviously tremendous rumours about the war. I will be quite honest – I had no idea there was going to be a war. In fact, I argued with my father all weekend that there was not going to be a war.

I could not believe that the lovely country I had just come back from and the super people that we had met, could possibly be at war, even though there was awful tension on the train between Basle and Strasbourg which ran parallel to the Maginot Line. The French really thought the Germans were going to attack that night, but still, I can honestly say, I really did not think the war would happen.

By the way, that two-week holiday in Austria cost £12.50. That was full board and all the travelling.

Why did I choose to go to Germany?

There was no deep philosophical reason why I went to visit Nazi Germany in August 1939 – the reason was that it was cheap. Cheaper than anywhere else in Europe. The possibility that a war might break out whilst I was on holiday did not come into it.

It was certainly cheap to go to Germany. Whereas the 'normal' exchange rate for German marks was 4DM to £1, travellers could get an exchange rate of 10DM to £1, as long as one bought it as Reiseschecks/travellers'

PHASE ONE

cheques. I see from the folder that only 10DM, in coinage, could be taken <u>into</u> Germany and all monies HAD to be declared. No German notes could be exported, which meant that all travellers' marks had to be spent. In the end, I had a wonderful time and war did <u>not</u> break out on my holiday!

On the Friday of that week, all clients of the advertising agency, for whom I was a production manager, started cancelling their advertisements. Starting early in the morning, people like Bowmans Furniture, Imperial Airways and Berger Paints cancelled, so that by the evening I just did not have any work to do at all.

Just then my mother phoned me from home to say, 'Vic, there is a telegram for you from the police. You are on duty tonight. Friday night, all night.'

So I said goodbye to Brumwell, the MD and Cox and all the friends at Stuart Advertising. I went home, had my tea and off I went to Harrow Road Police Station where they had my police uniform ready.

I was WRX 64. I was on duty that night with my uniform and with my gas mask. I really did not know what to expect.

My duty was 10 o'clock to 6 o'clock. That first Friday night we spent most of our time rushing around picking up drunks.

What is not realised these days is that, just before the war, on a Friday night in places like Shirland Road, Paddington, there were hundreds of drunks. The police were out in full force, bundling the drunks into the van and whipping them back to the police station to lock them up for the night. We forget what a tremendous difference there is in life between 1939 and 1996 with drugs, not drink.

So my first night on duty in the police was sorting out drunks and on the Saturday the same. At 6 o'clock on the Sunday morning when I clocked off, I went home to get to bed. At about 10.45 a.m. Dad came up to and said, 'I think you had better come down.' I put on my dressing gown and went downstairs to hear the broadcast by Chamberlain that the war had started. Almost immediately, the air-raid sirens went off – it was a mistake, it was just a private plane who had not informed aircraft control. Anyway, the air-raid sirens started and we all trooped into the shelter and thought that the war was going to start.

Many homes in London had a shelter in the back garden. They were called Anderson Shelters (after the Home Secretary at the time) and they were made of corrugated steel. They had to be dug deep into the ground.

The corrugated sides with a curve for the roof were fitted and then all the earth was put back on top. It made a fairly effective shelter and certainly saved many lives when the brutes actually came. But it was quite a shock to see Grandma, Mum and Aunt Mabel, my father's sister who lived with us, all getting into this air-raid shelter.

Dad, Doug (my younger brother) and I stood outside to look at the Spitfires which were sweeping around.

At 10 o'clock that night I was back on duty. We really did expect the German Luftwaffe to come flying in with its bombs and its gas. In those early days, we had to help the air-raid wardens with blackouts and make sure everybody switched their lights off. My dad spent the war as an Air Raid Warden and Mum was a 'fire watcher' and got a Defence Medal.

A funny anecdote – you may have heard of Flora Robson, the actress who played Queen Elizabeth in the film *Elizabeth of England*, she had left the light on in her flat. I was on duty and called for help. A couple of professional policemen came down and 'jemmied' open the door and switched out the lights.

In fact, the bombing did not start for nearly a year and I just did normal police work until I was called up on 19 October 1939.

Mostly, I was concerned with either drunks or prostitutes. For a shy 21-year-old that was quite an eye-opener. My beat happened to be along Randolph Avenue, Maida Vale, which was the red-light district.

Two little stories, one funny and one not so funny.

I had seen a drunk collapsed on the pavement and thought I had better take him in. So I went to the phone box to phone the police station to ask if they could send a van down to take him away. They said, 'No vans, sonny, bring him in.' So I went back to get him but he had gone. I thought, 'Oh blimey!, I'll make myself look a right Charlie if I phone up to tell them that I had lost my drunk.' I looked up the road and there he was. He had fallen over a hedge, one of these little privet hedges and was absolutely flat out. So I got him firmly by the hand, walked him back to the police station and charged him.

The next morning, he was up in the magistrates' court and I had to be there. He came up to me and he said, 'Are you the constable who brought me in last night?' I must admit I wondered what on earth he was going to say and I said, 'Well yes I am.' He said, 'I am grateful to you, because I just don't remember anything at all, I may well have had an accident and I'm thankful that you took me in.' He was fined 4s 6d.

PHASE ONE

The other episode was not quite so funny.

I was on duty during the daylight hours, because you did a month on and then you change shifts, and I was on the afternoon shift then, strolling down Scrubbs Lane towards North Pole Corner. There was a great shout and somebody came running saying that there had been an accident. I walked round and saw that a boy on a bike had managed to get himself right underneath an articulated lorry.

I was terrified. What on earth should I do?

The traffic was as far as you could see. Solid traffic and everybody honking on their horns. It was a shambles.

My heart died and suddenly I looked up and I could see the helmet of a real policeman coming down towards us. He arrived at the scene of the accident at the same time as I did. He said to me, 'Sonny, you look after the little boy under the lorry, the ambulance is coming. I'll deal with the driver of the lorry.'

So I said, 'but what about all the traffic?' and he put his head up and looked round as though for the very first time, he'd seen the traffic and he said, 'Oh fuck 'em!'

I went in the ambulance with the kid. Fortunately, he had managed to escape the wheels. He had gone right under the lorry and nothing had touched him. He was just badly shaken, thank goodness!

PHASE TWO

On 12 October 1939, I was ordered to report to Euston Station to join the Territorial Army, 2nd London Division. Euston is the station for the north and I expected to be sent to Scotland to start my training. I packed my suitcase, bid farewell to Mum and Dad and off I went to Euston Station where I reported to a room on Platform 5 and found that I was being put into the 140th Field Regiment of the Royal Artillery (Army Number 945215).

When about 20–30 of us had collected, the sergeant said, 'Right Oh, follow me,' and off we went. To my surprise, we went down into the Underground Railway. I thought, 'well, it seems we are not going on a train from Euston Station.' The tube train took us to Wood Green Station on the Piccadilly Line. There were lorries waiting outside and so we set off for Totteridge Green, near Finchley in north-west London.

The army had taken over a few private houses where we went to report. A very harassed-looking lieutenant said, 'What are you doing here?' and we said, 'We've been told to report to the 140th Field Regiment,' and he said, 'Oh, I don't know what to do with you. Go home and come back on Monday!'

So much for my first day in the army – I was home by 4 o'clock. Mum was surprised!

At 9 o'clock on Monday morning we all turned up at Totteridge to join the army; when asked, I said I had worked in an advertising agency, so the sergeant said, 'Oh you're a clerk.' I said, 'Well I've never actually seen myself as a clerk, but if you say so I suppose I am.'

'We need somebody in the regimental office,' he said. 'Off you go.' So I went upstairs and saw the regimental sergeant major.

PHASE TWO

The RSM really runs the office of the RHQ (Regimental Headquarters) so I joined the army and became an office clerk.

Life was very strange for me in those early days in the army; because I was such a fat lad (17½ stone) it was impossible for the army to fit me with the standard uniform and I had to continue wearing my civilian clothes. For lodgings, we just lived in local houses.

So having come out of the police force where I thought I was doing a really worthwhile job, I now found myself being a very second-rate office boy, living in a civilian house, working in civilian clothes in what was an office in a civilian house.

One point I must explain about wearing civilian clothes in a Territorial Army office. The unit I belonged to was the 140th Field Regiment of the Royal Artillery, a second-line unit to the 90th Field Regiment, RA. This was a well-trained unit with top men who, as soon as war started, went straight off to France with their super 25-pounder guns. The dregs were left behind to form a new unit.

The officers were too old, the sergeant majors were too old and some of the sergeants were far too young. These dregs of the Territorial Army, together with our group of 20-year-old militia made up the 140th Field Regiment, RA. But it was a dog's dinner of an army.

Because it was a TA unit, they normally had civilian clerks. Therefore, because I was in civilian clothes they thought I was a TA civilian clerk and did not realise I was a militia boy – so they called me 'Mr Markham'.

All the officers saluted when they came into the room. It was all quite amusing really.

They invited me to the officers' mess to do their books for them and gave me glasses of sherry. It was a very interesting time, but as I say, frustrating because I felt I had done a good job in the police force and I was just playing around in a silly little army.

Fortunately, the state of limbo only lasted about a month and in December we went off to Dursley in Gloucestershire, ostensibly to begin to be trained as soldiers.

At Dursley, we took over the offices and works of an old bedding company called Chapmans. From my point of view at least we (myself and two other clerks) had an office to work in and we really did work hard. We were doing twenty-four hours duty a day, living and sleeping in the office, seven days a week. We never had a moment off. We would sneak out in the evening to go and buy ourselves some fish and chips.

Most of the unit was a total shambles. We did not have guns, we did not have lorries; we did not have anything at all, just the men. We were supposed to form a full regiment of the Royal Artillery.

We had been ordered to start training men to drive lorries. The British School of Motoring came along with little Morris 8s and started to teach the men to drive.

We had no guns, so the men could not learn gunnery, and there were no rifles. The guard pickets went on duty with sticks and not guns; the only thing they could do was to spend their day marching up and down.

We were sent home on leave at Christmas. Then, after Christmas, surprise, surprise – I was given a form together with cloth and buttons and everything and told to go to a local civilian tailor to have a battle dress made to fit me.

Of course, the army being the army I had two battle dresses, two fatigue suits, the complete equipment. I think this civilian tailor got £2.16s for making up all these clothes.

It was now January 1939 and we still had no guns. The colonel, who was a very rich man, bought a few second-hand lorries and had them painted in khaki colour, so at least we had some kind of transport. This was very good because later in January we went to Larkhill, on Salisbury Plain, for a firing camp. They had four spare guns which they loaned to our regiment and each troop – a troop is four guns with three troops to a battery, two batteries to a regiment – had to borrow the guns in turn and fire them. The guns were 18-pounder Mark IV guns with a split trail and this was the first time these militia men and probably most of the TA men had ever fired a gun.

The next week we were sent home on 'embarkation leave'. I'll never forget, because it was one of the most poignant moments in my life, when my father, who had been all through the First World War, took me into the front room and quietly asked, 'Are you are going to France?' I replied, 'Well I am not supposed to say, but yes.' 'Best of luck son,' he said.

Afterwards, I thought constantly about what must he have thought having survived, miraculously, three years of the front line in the First World War. Now his son was going off to France to fight the battle that was not really finished in 1918. It must have been terrible for him.

After embarkation leave, we returned to Dursley to wait for our orders to come through. We did not have long to wait.

PHASE TWO

The first week in February, on a Wednesday, a sergeant came in and said, 'Well lads I hear we are going off to France on Saturday.' We all said, 'We can't be. We haven't got any guns and we haven't got any proper transport.'

'Well mark my words' he said, 'you'll be getting your orders soon.'

Sure enough, half an hour later in came the colonel and started issuing orders to everyone to get packed up and go to France.

Thursday came and we were all packing but still no guns or lorries.

Friday came, and then a most astonishing thing happened. Starting in the evening, an ATS driver came into the office and reported that she had brought a quad tractor with an ammunition limber and gun. Let me explain, this was the basic unit of a gun team.

'A quad tractor' really meant a four-wheel drive vehicle enclosed so the gun crew could sit inside to protect them from the rain. It was not armour plated at all. It had a 'gun platform' clamped on top. Behind the tractor was towed an ammunition limber and then a gun.

The gun really shook us. It was an 18-pounder Mark II field gun with a tubular trail. It looked like the guns used by the Royal Horse Artillery in their military drive at the Royal Tournament. Made in the USA in 1915, they were considered obsolete before the end of the First World War because the tubular trail used to warp if the gun was fired too much. These particular guns had been in Hong Kong and had been used to fire salutes to the governor. When the war started they were shipped home and these were the guns that we were given,

<u>A gun platform that never was</u>! After the First World War, in which tanks were used for the first time, it was deemed necessary for field guns, i.e. the guns we had, to be traversed (moved from side to side) quickly. To this end, a platform was devised, to which the gun was clamped, to allow easy traverse. The snag, so far as we were concerned, was that the platform was designed for the new 25-pounder gun/howitzer which our first-line regiment was issued with. The 18-pounder Mark II did not fit the platform, though they were issued to us. The quad tractor carried them around France, but we were never able to make use of them.

We were a Field Gun Unit assigned as anti-tank role 'Corps Troops', i.e. mobile troops to be put into a vital situation, to the BEF 1st Army Corps, attached to the 1st Division (the infantry unit HQ next to ours on the River Dyle were the Grenadier Guards). We were never issued with anti-tank ammunition – none was made for the 18-pounder gun. What a shambles!

The system was that all the gun crews, with their kit bags packed, should wait on the pavement, positioned about 10 yards apart, so that as the ATS girls with their quad tractors, ammunition and guns drove up from Birmingham, the girls would get out, the men would climb in and drive off up the road to position themselves ready for the convoy, due to start off at the crack of dawn, for France.

So the first time the drivers had driven such a strange vehicle was when they were going to France. Terrible really, but off we drove to Southampton.

In those days, of course, the ships were not roll-on, roll-off. Each vehicle had to be lifted by crane and put in the hold of the ship, which took a couple of days; on 9 February we set sail for France.

We had to put on our life jackets. Destroyers were dashing about and we made our way down past the Isle of Wight and across to Le Havre. It took all night, as it normally does, and we started the laborious task of unloading as soon as we landed. Fortunately, our office lorry was unloaded pretty quickly and off we went to Bolbec where we were to congregate to collect the whole regiment.

Let me explain about our vehicle. It was a Bedford lorry fitted out completely as an office, with filing trays and desks and room for a typewriter and a duplicating machine. It really was extremely useful for us.

It took a few days to get the regiment together. We were then issued with our movement orders. We were going to have a night convoy, the first night convoy we had ever done, up to the Belgian frontier. We had fifty vehicles in the convoy. The despatch riders spent their time dashing up and down the convoy trying to get everybody to keep together. We lost our first three men that night, despatch riders on motorbikes, killed when they got involved in accidents. It was a disaster.

There is a major problem with convoys. Although the driver in the front drives at a steady 30 miles per hour, the driver at the rear is either stopped or driving at 80 miles per hour in order to catch up. It is one of those weird things. Goodness knows why it happens, but it makes for absolute pandemonium.

At night, especially as we were not allowed to have our headlights on, because there was a war on and we may have been bombed, the vehicles in front had little red tail lights fitted underneath the vehicle so that you could just dimly see them through the gloom. Your own vehicles' headlights were just thin slits allowing them to shine a little bit ahead.

PHASE TWO

We drove through the night and our destination was a little village called Auchy near a larger town called Orchies. It is on the Route National 353 about a mile from the Belgian frontier.

We were there for about six weeks and it was a pretty frustration time as we were not allowed to use our guns because we were too near the Belgium frontier.

They laid on things for us: for example I went to Henin Leitard to hear Gracie Fields sing and a party of us drove to Lille twice a week. I was an extremely naïve 21-year-old. Most of the men went off to the brothels. I went to the cinema and saw the film *The Four Feathers*. I also used to go and buy egg and chips in the evening from the bar in the village. Nothing much happened.

What was extraordinary was that there we were, ostensibly in the front line, and nobody, but nobody wore their gas masks, whereas if you were home in London, a long way away from the front line, you had to wear your gas mask during air-raid alerts.

Officers were sent on training courses. One of them came back with what he thought was a strange story. He had been asked to plan an exercise to evacuate the British army through Dunkirk – somebody, somewhere was obviously thinking ahead.

After six weeks, 1st Corps HQ, to whom we were attached, thought it was about time that we began to train because, theoretically, we should not have been in France at all until we had been in the army for six months and been fully trained. As it was, we went to France before any training. The idea was that France was a big place, so we could start our training in France.

So off we went to a village between Doullens and Albert, called Villers Brettoneux. We had not been there long when an officer came into our office and said, 'Right, I've got a truck outside, would you like to come and see the First World War trenches?'

So would you believe it, here we were, young soldiers of the 1939 war, being taken off to the Somme to see the trenches and the war graves of the First World War.

When one comes to think about it, it was a pretty poignant moment, especially as three weeks later we were in the middle of it, fighting our own war.

We had hardly been training for a week before 10 May, the day that the Germans broke through into Holland and the day that the phoney war finally ended and the real war started.

PHASE THREE

I was woken at about 5 o'clock in the morning by the sound of bombing. The other fellows in the room, about ten of them, could hear bombs dropping at Doullens just a few miles away.

I was terrified. This was the first time that I had heard bombing, and I was really scared.

I remember that everybody else was smoking and as I had never smoked in my life I thought, 'Well may be this is a good time to start.' We were issued with hundreds of cigarettes and I remember picking up a cigarette, lighting it, and beginning to puff. I thought, 'This is stupid, it tastes so awful and it's burning my mouth and not doing me any good at all.' I threw it away and I have never smoked since.

Very shortly afterwards, the regimental sergeant major started getting things organised and I went to the office truck and we packed up for battle. The RSM, an old sweat from the First World War, made us fill a cupboard with tins of food and how right he was – it came in very useful later.

It took the rest of the day to get things sorted out and in the evening we drove off to war. Before we started, the colonel called us together and told us that this was the big battle and we were going forward into Belgium to meet the Germans.

We drove all night through Belgium, arriving in Brussels in the early morning. As our unit was completely motorised we were ordered to drive through. The people acted as if we were liberating them; they showered us with food and champagne and it was quite shattering.

PHASE THREE

The vehicles were eventually parked for the night in one of the long avenues in Brussels. It looked towards the Royal Palace and was lined with chestnut trees, rather like the Champs Elysee in Paris. All the vehicles were put under these trees with the guns and everything, while the men of the unit went off to have a gay old time in Brussels. Again, being the naïve youngster that I was, I stayed put in the office vehicle.

At about 1 o'clock in the morning, there was a great hullabaloo because we had received orders to go straight to the front line. There just weren't any drivers. We managed to scout around and, in regimental headquarters, we found one lad who had learnt to drive but had never driven a lorry before. But at least he was a driver and he promised to drive the office truck. By and large, we found just about enough people to drive the guns and the lorries up to the front line. At 2 o'clock in the morning we were near Wavre on the River Dyle. We could hear the guns firing – they were German guns. It was absolutely terrifying. I mean, here we were without any gunners, without any staff, and just enough men to get the vehicles into position in the front line. The RSM had to get all the spare lorries and bring the men up the next morning – dragging them out of the brothels and out of the bars. What a shambles.

When you consider that our men had only fired their guns on a training exercise for a week, probably not more than just a couple of times, and now here we were in action on the River Dyle against the German army who had just smashed through the Belgian army and, previously, the Polish army.

We were there to stop them. At least that is what we thought. Of course, we were quite wrong, we had been led into a trap.

The reason why we had not been bombed on the way into Belgium was because the Germans wanted to draw us into Belgium so that when they made their breakthrough at Sedan, and came around the back of us, we would be cut off. And that is just how it happened.

On the River Dyle we parked our office truck in a wood. We dug a slit trench as an air-raid shelter. There was a big farmhouse nearby that the officers used. We found another farmhouse nearby which we could use for sleeping.

We were bombed. It was our first experience of being bombed. You could see the bomb bays open as the Heinkel III bombers, coming directly towards us only a few hundred feet up, swept over and dropped their bombs.

We looked up in terror as these black shapes hurtled towards us. Had they hit the slip trench they would have killed us all. As it was, the wind carried the bombs 50 yards to our left into a road which was full of refugees. Quite obviously, with hindsight, it was the refugees and not us that the bombers were targeting.

I saw a British Lysander being chased by a Messerschmitt 109 until it was shot down.

I was on guard duty that night, a most extraordinary experience. The whole of the night sky was lit with the flashes of the guns on both sides. The whole earth trembled with the sound of the field guns, the screaming chatter of the German Spandau machine guns and the slow toc-a-toc of the British Vickers machine guns. This went on non-stop until 16 May.

Our positions were good ones. Our observers could see over the river well into the German positions. What they reported back was quite extraordinary. Our field guns, as I have already mentioned, were motorised, but the German artillery was horse drawn, just as it was in the First World War. Our guns caused carnage amongst the German gun crews and horses.

We could have held these positions for a long time. However, in regimental headquarters we heard that the Germans had broken through on the right flank and we had to retreat. RHQ had to issue orders so that the regiment could get out of this front-line position.

Our unit was to act as a rear guard on the right flank to protect the British Expeditionary Force as it retreated. At that very moment, the German artillery started ranging on us and the wood in which we were based. That was a really anxious moment.

Fred Pitt, the other clerk, and I had to sit there while we typed out and ran off, on the Roneo, the movement orders for the regiment. Trees were falling around us, shells were exploding around us. We just had to sit there and take it.

Everybody else had rushed off to the slit trenches to protect themselves, but there was no way we could protect ourselves. If we went for protection then we could not type out the orders and the regiment could not move, meaning the regiment would have to stay until such time as we issued the orders. So we just sat it out in all this shell fire and got the orders run off. My hands were trembling.

One rather amusing item – in the middle of all this I was bursting for a pee. Can you imagine how idiotic it is standing up peeing against a tree

PHASE THREE

which might at any moment be blown up by a shell. You think to yourself, 'Well I have got to pee.' I often wonder how many people get killed having a pee.

At last we got the orders typed, run off on the Roneo and set out by the despatch riders. Don Rs we called them.

We locked up the office and drove off. The driver was panic stricken. He swept round so quickly that everything, but everything, flew off the lorry onto the ground. The sergeant major yelled at me, 'Markham you pick it all up and follow us with a Don R. So I had, in the midst of all this shelling, to pick up all these secret documents, put them under my arm, grab a despatch rider, sit on the pillion and chase after our office lorry. I jumped on the back of the motorbike, clutched the lad round the middle and off we went! He roared up the middle of the road and suddenly round the corner, they were little windy roads like you get in Devon, there was a huge Scammell lorry coming towards us to pick up one of the big heavy guns. How we got from under those wheels I will never know.

Anyway, we soon caught up with the office truck and off we started in the great retreat. We drove across Belgium towards France.

The Germans were attacking through Belgium and the British Expeditionary Force were deployed at the River Dyle. But further south the Germans broke through at Sedan to get to the Channel ports to cut off the British Expeditionary Force, so that this force of some 250,000 would be captured.

We did not know this plan at the time of course. We thought that the main thrust of the German army was still through Belgium and as we retreated the Germans attacked very vigorously.

Our field guns were spending most of the time firing at what is called 'open sights', which means point-blank aims at German infantry advancing across fields. The gun crews would wait until the last moment and then the guns would be hooked up to their tractors and roar off. This meant that in our trucks we often overtook very tired British infantry. We took up new positions and hoped that the British infantry would pass through our lines to continue their retreat.

It was a terrible time, honestly.

We were, fortunately, in our vehicles.

I vividly remember watching troops sleepwalking along the road, sometimes leaning on the man in front, trailing their rifles, just dragging them along the ground, hardly being able to put one foot in front of the other they were so tired and exhausted.

The retreat went on for three days until 19 May and our unit finished up just outside Tournai. It is on the River Escaut which ultimately leads down to the Rhine. We were at a little village just outside Tournai overlooking the river towards the attacking Germans.

It was a very fierce battle and we were under continuous shell fire for three days, night and day.

The interesting point about a battle for a town is that the air is full of paper floating about. I presumed people were burning it and it swept up into the air. It may have come from offices which had been bombed.

During this time, I had a couple of very narrow escapes.

On one occasion I was walking across a field near our headquarters with two other men when suddenly a Messerschmitt 109 swooped down, swung round two or three times and machine-gunned the field to try to kill us. We ran for our lives and dashed into a ditch. It was a very hair-raising episode I can assure you.

The second was quite extraordinary. As I said, we had been shelled for three days continuously. I remember one night vividly when we all woke up and wondered what had happened and we realised they had stopped shelling. For the first time there was no noise and it had woken us up. That was most odd.

It was at this time that our colonel realised that we hadn't any maps of the area, so I was given a lorry and a driver and told to go back to Arras, which was the main headquarters of the BEF, to see if I could get some maps. So off we went. When we got there, to my surprise, the place seemed deserted. In fact, as we got to the bridge a Royal Engineers officer stopped us and said, 'What are you doing here?'

I explained that I had orders to go into General Headquarters to get some maps.

He said, 'You won't find anybody there I'm sure.' I said, 'I have been ordered to go to GHQ by my colonel.' He said, 'Well you had better hurry up because I am going to blow up this bridge. The Germans are on the other side of the town.' So we drove on to GHQ to find that the whole of the headquarters was empty and there was no possibility of getting any maps.

So we turned round to go back again. As we drove over the bridge, the officer blew it up behind us. It was quite extraordinary.

PHASE THREE

So here we had a situation: the Germans, in Arras, were behind us and we were moving back to the so-called 'front' – so we had Germans on both sides of us.

When I got back and reported this to the RHQ they were all shattered.

A final interesting point. As we approached RHQ on our return, the shelling on either side of the road was intense and we stopped the truck 100 yards away for a moment, just to look. I remember thinking to myself, 'We must be stark raving mad. Here we are quite safe and yet deliberately we are driving along this road towards all this mayhem and shelling.'

It is odd the things you do in the war. You do them not because you <u>want</u> to do them, not because you <u>have</u> to do them; you do them because you feel it is the right thing to do, because others <u>expect</u> you to do them.

Just after my return, the unit started to take casualties, though fortunately not in regimental headquarters.

As well as being a clerk in the office I was also a stretcher bearer when we got into action, but fortunately, up to then I had not had to do any stretcher bearing.

The unit then had orders to withdraw to Cassel. It took a day or so and we went through the Forest of Nieppe where we were badly bombed by Stukas.

Being involved in a retreat is a terrifying experience. The Belgians were retreating with us on the roads and they were fleeing from their homes. Their fear was awful. They were wondering what was going to happen to them because they knew of the atrocities of the First World War.

The roads were full of cars and horse and carts, laden to the eyeballs, with everything that people could load on to them. Fleeing in front of the Germans.

They were machine-gunned from the air. They were bombed from the air, not only at high level but at low level by Stukas, and Junker 87s, which had screaming devices fitted to their wings. As one dived every single person felt it was coming straight at them. It was a terrifying experience.

People were pushing and shoving. Old ladies and children were screaming and people were being pushed off the road. Horses were dying. What a shambles.

The fields too were full of cows that had not been milked, many were bellowing and many were dead. The stink and the smell of dead bodies was everywhere.

At about that time, the army was in such a confused state that it could not supply us with rations so that from 22 May we did not get an official ration at all, we had to live off the land, which meant stealing.

We eventually arrived at Cassel, a town on the main road to Dunkirk. Being on top of a hill, it dominates the whole area.

We could see Dunkirk quite clearly from the top of the hill. It was a very important position.

During the First World War, the British army had its headquarters there, especially during the Battle of Passchendaele. This was a battle in which my father participated. It is quite likely that he was in Cassel too, which is a most odd thought.

Cassel is also a junction for five major roads, so it was a very vital town for the Germans to take. The British army recognised this, so the 145th Brigade of the 48th Division were detailed to protect Cassel from the Germans. To defend it at all costs.

The 48th Division was led by a Major General Thorne, the 145th Brigade was led by Brigadier Nigel Somersct and the brigade consisted of the Oxon and Bucks Light Infantry, the Gloucester Regiment, the Warwickshire Regiment and two batteries of artillery.

I should explain. The 140th Field Regiment consisted of two batteries: 366 and 367. They tossed up to see who was to stay behind and who was to go home; 366 won and 367 stayed behind.

Regimental headquarters were to stay behind anyway, so we did not have any choice.

The other unit that stayed behind was Kings Troop of the Royal Horse Artillery, although they did not have their horses. Kings Troop is the one that gallops round at the Royal Tournament every year, so we were in very distinguished company.

At first our unit did not go straight up to the top of the hill at Cassel. 367 battery and the regimental headquarters were based at the bottom of the hill on the Hazebrouck Road.

The road is numbered D53. It was a quite narrow, tree-lined, road with a ditch. There was a big house which had just been vacated by General Gort, the general in command BEF, who had had a meeting with the French generals. It lay about 50 yards back from the road. Leading up to it were big iron gates on the road side.

PHASE THREE

As soon as we arrived, we switched on the radio to get the news. Rather ominously, we heard the king had called the nation to a day of prayer FOR US! We didn't much like the sound of that.

Our major, who was second in command, expected the German tanks to come down this little road from Hazebrouck and he positioned one of our 18-pound guns on the roadway and put the RHQ staff in the ditch by the side. There were about nine of us in this ditch.

We had a Boys anti-tank rifle, which was a disaster, and an old Lewis machine gun. The machine gun was right next to me.

Early in the morning we were dive-bombed, nothing very serious.

Later on, I heard a strange noise. I could hear tractors, what I thought were farm tractors, and I thought that it was odd with the war almost on our doorstep that some farmer could still be ploughing up his field.

Remember, we were in a ditch on the right-hand side of the road, facing towards Hazebrouck. The road turned left at a corner about 200 yards ahead. On my immediate left was the 18-pound field gun, stationed in the road. On my right was an open field with hedges about 100 yards away. In this field there was a Bofors anti-aircraft gun facing the sky. To my immediate right, about 10 yards away, was a 2-pound light anti-tank gun covering this area. Laying in the ditch were the eight other men of RHQ and right next to me a lance bombardier with the Lewis machine gun.

Then drama. Simultaneously two things happened.

First of all, round the corner facing us from Hazebrouck came a British army truck towing a 2-pound anti-tank gun. At that moment, it was hit by a German mortar shell which exploded and set the tyres of the gun on fire. The lorry drove, very fast, towards us with the driver and the passenger leaning out of the windows and shrieking, 'The Germans are coming, the Germans are coming,' and roared past us at a rate of knots with the wheels of the tyres spinning like a Catherine wheel with fire and sparks flying everywhere.

It was somewhat disturbing!

The next thing that happened was a German spotter plane, a Fieseler Storch, came flying over very low in order to spot for the German mortar. The Bofors gunners very bravely opened fire and it became a battle between the gun trying to shoot down the plane and the plane directing the mortar fire onto the gun. The mortar, unfortunately, won with a direct hit and every man on the gun team was killed. So that was the end of that defence.

Next, mortar bombs began falling, with great accuracy, into the ditch where we were sheltering. Starting off at the corner of the road where the British anti-tank gun had been hit, the tank advanced slowly, the bombs exploding at 10-yard intervals as it moved towards us. Nearer and nearer they fell, with big explosions. We were just mesmerised! We did not know what to do … We could not run away. So we just lay there hoping for the best.

As I have already said, the road was lined with trees which grew beside the ditch and, fortunately for me, the mortar shell fell just the other side of the tree nearest to me. The next shell fell on the other side of the next tree down the road towards Cassel, leaving me unscathed. I had, in artillery terms, been bracketed. To say that I had been terrified would be an understatement.

Although I did not realise it at the time, the sergeant in charge of the anti-tank gun on my immediate right took fright, packed up and fled and did not tell us. So that flank-covering fire was left open. After a few moments, we realised how right he was to get away, because the so-called tractor burst through the hedge, and of course it wasn't a tractor at all, it was two German Panzer Mk IIs. They burst through the hedge and made towards us. Next to me the bombardier with the Lewis machine gun opened fire. The young sergeant with the field gun in the road, very quickly sized up the situation and very bravely swung the gun round to point towards the tank – this was the moment that the gun platform should have been used, if it had fitted the 18-pounder, and began to fire on the tank.

The guns were supposed to be in an anti-tank role, but we did not have armour-piercing shells. We only had high-explosive shells that just went bang. We hoped they would frighten them off.

The tank kept coming towards us firing at the gun and at our ditch. The gun was firing at the tank and if you can imagine, as it was only a narrow road the muzzle of the gun was immediately above my head and, as it fired, the hot blast from the end of the gun scorched the back of my neck.

I was crouching in this ditch with the top of the ditch being taken off by the machine gun from the tank. The man next to me who was firing the Lewis gun was killed. I am afraid I was desperately cowardly.

Before I knew what had happened, another senior man came dashing over the road, jumped into the ditch, took the machine gun and started firing

PHASE THREE

at the tank for about five seconds until he too was killed. Both these chaps were actually touching my shoulder. Fortunately, the Germans in the tanks thought better of it and reversed and went back through the hedge. I was totally deafened, my ear drum shattered, in a complete daze and terrified throughout this action.

What I found very strange indeed was just sitting there doing nothing. For years, as a Scout, I had been in a position to lead my patrol of nine lads, or, finally, as Troop Leader, lead a troop of thirty-six lads. 'Leadership' was what my life had been about. It was therefore, terribly difficult <u>not</u> to give a lead under this extraordinary situation. I felt a tremendous urge to stand up and say 'Come on, move out!'

But I was nobody – I had absolutely no authority at all. I was a 'gunner', the lowest form of animal life, and the only person I was responsible for was <u>me</u>. So feeling terrible about it, I kept my head down.

A lieutenant gave an order and everyone got up and ran towards the chateau at our back, leaving our dead behind us. The machine guns were still firing from the tanks. We rushed towards the big house, got inside, went up on to the first floor and leaned out of the window, firing with everything we had at the four German tanks we could now see, to try to drive them away. They must have been as scared as we were, because eventually they all went away.

I don't suppose the whole thing lasted more than half an hour, but it was half an hour of the most terrifying fear and anguish.

It was decided then that we would all make for Cassel proper. We had to leave the guns and our equipment and go by the road in our lorry. There was no other way.

The crossroads were covered by the Germans, so we had to go through a barrage of machine-gun fire to get to Cassel. We waited until nightfall and then roared along the road and dashed into Cassel. Fortunately, no one in our truck was hurt.

<u>Then came the nightmare of Cassel itself</u>. As I have explained, the town dominates the whole area. We were billeted in a house, which, like all French houses, had an underground cellar. Se we were quite safe while we were in the cellar. I was detailed to act as a runner between our RGH and brigade headquarters, which was in the castle in Cassel.

There was no electric light. It was just like a picture out of *Journey's End* with candles guttering, the place trembling to the shells, sandbags over the windows, shaking as the shell blast blew through the window. Officers limping in with blood pouring down as they leant over a map explaining what the latest position was.

As a runner I was sent off to the Warwickshire Regiment – an infantry regiment with Vickers machine guns. The officer was terribly casual and took me round and showed me the Vickers gun which was dominating the whole area. I could see Dunkirk quite clearly just 20 miles away. It was burning and the smoke from the burning oil tanks spread for miles.

Acting as a runner is quite a thing. You have to listen out for the shells. If one is coming you duck into a doorway. When you don't think one is coming, you run to the next doorway.

I remember with horror, in one doorway, a militia mate of mine had not been quite quick enough and he was laying on the step with his guts ripped open by the shrapnel from a shell. He was dying. I remember holding him in my arms and trying to comfort him, but what comfort can you give a man with his guts ripped out. He did not take long to die.

Suddenly it was discovered that we might have to retreat to Dunkirk and we had not got any maps. So I was told to trace a map – would you believe that? I set myself up in one of the rooms with a desk right up against the window so that I could get as much light as possible. I was tracing this map with my head almost touching the window. Outside on the other side of the window, literally 3 feet away if that, was a major of our unit.

I must explain that the colonel had been injured the day before and had been sent home so that the major, who was second in command, had taken over. He was outside yelling instructions and I could hear a shell coming. I stood back from the window.

The window shattered. The glass and shrapnel came across the desk and the major outside was badly wounded. I rushed out and helped the stretcher bearers to carry him back to the CCS – the casualty clearing station.

That was another narrow escape for me.

That evening, what was left of the brigade paraded in the square. There was only a handful of men, because by that time, every single one of our guns on the hill had been destroyed, together with their gun crews, and the infantry units had taken a terrible battering.

One of the officers stood up and made a speech. He said, 'We are going to try to break through to Dunkirk. You mustn't fire rifles or make any noise at all. We've to try and sneak through the German lines.' We were shown details of the position of the BEF.

PHASE THREE

'If you walk down to the bottom of the hill' he said, 'there is a sergeant there, he'll tell you what to do. You will crawl on your hands and knees and hope to be able to crawl through the German lines. The Gloucester Regiment, with their machine guns, are going to stay behind and fire over our heads to make the Germans think that we are still here.'

I can tell you honestly, I did not think for one moment that I would be taken prisoner of war. It never occurred to me that such a thing would happen. I thought that we would make it. How naïve can you get?

Anyway, down the hill we went. It was dark and all around us we could hear the German tanks. The villages were being set on fire, German Verey lights were being fired. The German artillery was in action and our machine guns were firing over our heads, vigorously, to make out that we were really defending Cassel.

We crawled and we crawled. Nose to tail! We did not make a sound. All around us there was the most frightful mayhem going on; the Germans were blowing the place up.

I suppose it was about 4 or 5 o'clock that dawn broke. You know what dawn is like on a spring morning – cold but with a morning mist. So you could not see in front of you, but if we looked up we could see the German spotter planes just above us.

We all gathered together in little minor roads. There were very few officers and nobody knew anything. Up ahead we could see a crossroads and when we got there we found that it said Cassel to our left 4 kilometres. That was not much for a night's crawl.

What we did not realise was that 4 kilometres put us very firmly in the German artillery lines. The first thing that happened was that a German machine gun opened up on us. We all ducked for shelter behind a stone wall and then somebody decided that we ought to take this machine gun out.

I suppose that there were about 300 of us at this moment.

Some of the infantry had their rifles, but because in RHQ we did not have a rifle or anything, we were completely unarmed. I merely had a satchel over my shoulder with some field dressings.

We all walked across the field towards this machine gun. It was most strange. One does not hesitate to stand up from the shelter of a stone wall to walk, unprotected, across a field, all mates together. You can't let them down. You would feel such a twit staying, crouched behind the wall, with everyone else moving forward.

The Germans were alternating ordinary and tracer (fiery) tracer bullets and you could see the bullets going across the field. You were walking across the field and you just, sort of, seemed to walk between the bullets.

Most strange. In fact, the whole thing was odd, in that you did not realise you were there, you felt that you were watching a film. Today I suppose you would say you were watching the telly, but in those days if felt that you were not actually physically there. That you were standing back seeing it all happening. This must be the self-protection that we give ourselves, otherwise, we would all go stark raving mad under those conditions.

Anyway, someone put the machine gun out of action. Then suddenly, to our surprise, one of our own quad tractors with a limber and a gun turned up. We did not know we had any left undamaged. It was trying to make its way through to Dunkirk on this minor road.

So, we thought, super, put it up in the front and we will follow behind. And we marched off down this very narrow, little country lane. It had ditches on either side with a hedge on the right-hand side and a high bank on the left. It was like a gully really.

We tried to squeeze up tight against the tractor to get some kind of protection. Spirits were up. We thought, right we are on the way to Dunkirk and so off we went. I suppose I was about 25 yards from the quad tractor. Everybody, solid, in between me and that. The sky and the morning mist had lifted, the road bent round to the left, everyone was excited and rushing down the road.

And then, horror! Suddenly the quad tractor halted.

Everyone yelled, 'Go On, Go On,' and then all hell hit it.

One hundred yards away, in the roadway, was a German field gun. It fired at point blank range, blowing the tractor to smithereens; the ammunition limber exploded. They still kept on, firing down the road.

The killing field finished about 10 yards in front of me. It was horrific.

A solid mass of men, absolutely wiped out. Burnt and shrivelled and bits blown off everywhere. It was terrifying. I just dived for the ditch at the side of the road.

I remember vividly this red-hot shell, about 3 feet up, tearing down the road and exploding further behind us.

There were tanks everywhere and they opened up with their machine guns, bullets were zipping everywhere. One just zipped past my right ear,

PHASE THREE

sending up dirt on to the side of my face. The chap just in front of me in this ditch was killed, there were bodies everywhere. It was absolutely horrific.

This kept up for, I suppose, a few minutes, but it seemed like a lifetime.

Then there was silence, if you could discount all the screams and shouts of the wounded.

A chap, a British lad, walked down the road from the German lines with a white hanky in his hand.

Opposite the road to me was our major from 369 Battery who had taken over command of what was left of the regiment. He was the third commander we had had in three days. He had got both his legs blown off. I later carried him in, and he died that morning.

The chap with the hanky said, 'The Germans tell us that we ought to pack it in.'

The major said, 'Yes, surrender.'

This was the moment that we stood up with our hands up and slowly walked down the road, towards the German soldiers heavily armed with machine guns, tanks and a field gun.

PHASE FOUR

On 30 May 1940, the Germans greeted us with, 'Ah ha, Tommy, for you the war is over. In three weeks, we shall be in England.' Frankly, I had no reason to disbelieve them.

They were smart-looking soldiers. In their black uniforms with the death's head and the word *Totenkopf* embroidered on their sleeves, these were our captors.

Without doubt, the moment of capture was the most traumatic experience of my life.

This was the morning of 30 May. We had started action on 10 May, so we had only been in action for three weeks, but it was three intensive weeks. There was hardly a moment that we were not being bombed or shelled or machine-gunned.

We'd had very little sleep and towards the end we'd had very little food. So we were in a pretty shattered state.

And then this desperate business of the morning. The blowing up of the quad tractor with the swathe of death behind it. The dash into the ditch, with all the machine-gun bullets being sprayed down both ditches and people being killed. In the midst of all this mayhem and death, I was not even scratched. It was almost unbelievable.

The shock to the system was such that everything that happened in my life after that moment was as though it happened for the first time.

I remember later on in Camp 12 that I had a piece of chocolate given to me and it was as though it was the first time in my life I had ever tasted chocolate. A whole host of experiences from then on: the beauty of the

PHASE FOUR

clouds; the green of the fields; the rain; the sun. It was as though it was a watershed in my life. That I should have died and I did not. From that moment on, my life was as though it had started again. It was quite an extraordinary feeling.

The Totenkopf Division of the SS who captured us had a notorious record.

In fact, there is a book, which I have, called *Death on the Road to Dunkirk*, which says that this same Totenkopf Division murdered a lot of British soldiers earlier that morning.

What was strange was that they had said to us, 'You are very lucky to be taken prisoner of war because earlier this morning a group of your friends came towards us and at the last moment a sergeant major, who had his hands up, had a grenade in his hand and he threw it and killed some of our comrades. And our comrades killed everybody there.'

Whether it was the men who captured us or another group in a different company I will never know. All I can say is they were very correct with us. They did not mistreat us at all. There was no bullying or pushing.

My first task of course, as a stretcher bearer, was to help bring in all the wounded.

There was a barn there and the German doctors were working hard. I went back to get our major. As I have said, he was our third commander in three days and now he was dying.

Later on, there was no more stretcher bearing to do.

As I did not have any medical skills at that time, I was just herded back with the other prisoners of war into a field. We stayed there practically the whole day waiting for them to collect bits and bobs of POWs from all around until they had got 200–300 of us in the field.

It seemed to be all that was left of the brigade. Then they marched us to Steenvoode, the nearest town, where we stayed the night. We sat in the market place and just went to sleep where we sat.

The next day, we marched to Hazebrouck and went into what had been a French army barracks. They gave us a handful of what looked like little dog biscuits. That was the only food we had had for two days. They also managed to bring us some water.

On the march from Steenvoode to Hazebrouck we had to pass Cassel. We could see it on our right as we walked down the road. It was a most strange experience.

The business of being captured and herded together and marched down the road with a tank at the front and a tank at the back to make sure we did not escape.

The impact on my parents

They had received letters, regularly, from me since my arrival in France in February. From 10 May onwards we did not have the time or the opportunity to write. Nevertheless, the papers at home were full of what was happening.

When men started to come home from Dunkirk, my dad did everything in his power to try to discover where I was. Then the scout leader of the 28th Willesden Scouts, Mr Edward D. Stember, somehow found a sergeant major from our unit who had driven up on his motorbike from our Wagon-Lines (Quartermaster's stores) to the front line to discover what was going on. As he neared the front line he was fired on by a German machine gun. He quickly swung the motorbike around and fled back to report that our guns had been overrun and that we must have been taken POW – in fact of course, that was not so and we were not taken POW for another five days.

So, Mum and Dad assumed that I was a POW.

However, it took a month to get the official news from the War Office that I was 'missing'. They also had a Roneoed form sent to them explaining how the War Office were trying to ascertain if I was a POW.

And so we started on our march into Germany. The march started at Hazebrouck, then we went on to Lillers, St Pol, Hesdin and then to Doullens. From Doullens to Bapaume and then from Bapaume to Cambrai – about 200 kilometres.

It was very, very hot.

Each evening they gave us food and water.

It was a different type of German who was guarding us now. They were called Pioneers. They were grubby people.

Because we were front-line troops they beat us and shot at us and many men were killed on the march. Lorries would run us down and no bother to stop. French women would put out food or water for us to drink and the Germans would kick it all over. Just one example of their attitude towards us.

PHASE FOUR

One of the men in my office, Fred Pitt, had been slightly injured in the hand, not enough to stop him marching, but his hand started swelling up and it was very painful and it made him slow down on the march. So I, with my stretcher bearer's armband, marched with him and slowly, slowly, slowly, we got to the end of the column and then slowly, slowly, slowly, we fell further behind the column.

A German guard stayed with us because he wanted us to keep up with the column and he beat me with his rifle. He held the rifle by the muzzle and just kept on swinging it. At the end of each swing, boomph, in the middle of my back. He knocked my helmet off and would not let me stop to pick it up. I just had to keep on walking with Fred. He tried to make me run ahead and I wouldn't, I just kept walking with Fred.

I must admit he did not try to hit Fred – it was just me he hit. Some of these guards were shooting men who dropped behind and maybe he felt he could not get away with that because there were two of us. But the whole day he beat me with that rifle and my back was bruised black and blue.

At Doullens they put us under cover in an old prison (my dad, in his notes, calls it The 'Citadel') for the night, but most nights we just stayed out in the fields. We literally walked in, in our uniforms, got into the field and dropped exhausted. We slept in the field until the next day, sometimes in the rain, then off we went again.

Because I had a stretcher bearer's armband on, I was called over, at one time, because there was a chap moaning and groaning and the Germans thought that he was dying and I was asked if I would look at him. He was just trying to pull a fast one, you know how they do. They try to make a bit of fuss. There wasn't anything wrong with him. So I kicked him and said, 'You march you bugger, like everybody else.' He did.

The stench of death all around us was the awful thing. This march we were making was along the route the Germans had made moving into France. The bodies and the stench of the animals and people still left by the side of the road stayed in your nostrils for weeks.

Funnily enough, once you go without food for three or four days or more, you do not seem to need it. Just towards the end of this march, the Germans suddenly found they had got enough soup to give us two helpings but I could not eat it. Most strange.

At Cambrai they took us to the railway station and put us on a train. It was quite an interesting train journey.

NO ESCAPE: THE MEMOIRS OF A POW IN STALAG XXA

To start with they put us in open cattle trucks and we were packed in so closely that there was no way we could sit down. We were all wedged in so tight that we could only stand up and look over the edge of the cattle truck. It was very tiring just standing up all the time.

As the train shunted forwards and backwards we got pushed here and there. I remember vividly that first night in the train. It stopped in a siding and just stayed there all night and that was how we slept – all standing up.

One fellow wanted to go for a shit and needed to take his trousers down. He climbed out of the truck and sat astride the rails, one foot on either side of the rails. Without warning, the train was shunted by another train. It just pushed forward and split him down the middle.

The next morning, they drove us onto the other track and then reversed so that we were in exactly the same spot. Men came along with shovels and shovelled him away.

That was a pretty harsh way of dying wasn't it?

Anyway, the next day they put us onto a different train. It was a flat, the things that they had used to bring up the tanks. We sat down this time. That was quite comfortable. We had the most gorgeous journey through the Ardennes. You could see everywhere around. The train did not go very fast, it just trundled along through the most beautiful country.

I think it is a bit strange, that here we were as prisoners of war and we could still, if we wanted to, enjoy the beauty of the countryside. I most certainly did. I remember it vividly. We went through Dinant and Namur to Luxembourg.

Now that was strange, because on my holiday in Germany in August we had stopped in Luxembourg station to have a meal in the restaurant. A very good meal. By a strange coincidence, the truck I was in, stopped exactly opposite this restaurant.

We had not been fed at all on the railway train. We were absolutely starving and I could look over the track and see into this restaurant where, only a few months before, I had had a good meal. Such is the way of fate!

Trier was our first stop in Germany. It was a big camp on top of the hill. We could hardly drag ourselves up the hill what with the lack of food and water, and dysentery.

Getting drinking water had been a problem on the march. Whenever we saw a river we would lean down and drink out of it. Only there were dead bodies floating down the river. People, horses and other animals.

PHASE FOUR

Or, if we passed a field with swedes or turnips or potatoes, we would rush in and try and grab some before the Germans forced us back.

So our stomachs were in a terrible condition.

When we finally got to the top of the hill we sat down exhausted. A corporal came over and said, 'Are there any medical orderlies here, because we need help in the hospital?'

By coincidence I was sitting next to fifty or sixty Royal Army Medical Corps personnel. They must have captured a complete field ambulance. The sergeant major stood and said, 'No one here will volunteer. I want you all to be kept together.'

So I stood up and said, 'Well, I am only a stretcher bearer, but if I can be of any use I will volunteer to help.' 'Oh good,' he said, 'come on then,' and took me over to the hospital hut.

As I have explained, this terrible food and dirty water that we had been drinking had caused awful stomach trouble. Scores of men had got dysentery and were literally shitting themselves to death.

In the hut were about thirty men. They were lying, without blankets, on bunk beds. In the room were buckets for them to shit into. Some of them could not make it and there was shit, slime and blood all over the floor.

I was told that my job was to scrub the floor, three times a day with chloride of lime and water. I swilled the place and sprinkled the chloride of lime and brushed it in and then washed the whole thing down. It was not a particularly pleasant job, but it had to be done and I was a stretcher bearer, and so I did it.

A few days later, when the men were in a better condition, I was told to give out medicines and act as a medical orderly.

What happened next was one of those strange events of the Nazi era. In charge of the administration of the hospital was a German *sanitater* – that is the name for a German medical orderly. His task was to look after us and the hospital. One day he wanted something brought back to the hut. He called me over and said, 'Come with me, come Tommy' – that is how they used to speak to the British – and off we went round the camp to get whatever it was that he wanted me to bring back.

As we walked along, we came across a little old man sweeping the path. As this tall, hefty German *sanitater* went by he kicked him firmly up the arse and turned round to me and said, 'Well, you have a go, go on, he's only a Jew. You have a go.'

I said, 'No thank you.'

For goodness sake! The German thought I was a bit strange not wanting to kick this Jew up the arse. That is how the Germans used to treat the Jews. They called them the *untermenschen*, (the under-peoples). If you saw one you kicked them, and he saw him and he kicked him.

So much for Nazi Germany.

Another strange thing that happened a day or so later was that one of the medical orderlies in this hospital, a sergeant, said to me, 'Have you got the Geneva Convention bit written in your pay book?'

I did not know what he was talking about. In the slap-happy unit I belonged to, nothing like that happened properly.

He said, 'Well, if you are a stretcher bearer and you obviously are, then you should have had written in your pay book to the effect that you are covered by the Geneva Convention.' So he said, 'Give the pay book to me and I will write it in for you.'

So he wrote it in and signed the name of the regimental doctor. It was a poor bit of forgery, but what the heck. It saved my bacon from then on. If I had not had it written in I would not have been accepted as a medical orderly later on.

I managed to borrow a razor and razor blade from someone and I had a wash and a shave, the first one since I was captured.

When I'd joined the army, I'd been a big fellow, I weighed 17½ stone – now I was down to 11 stone, so when I had washed myself and put my glasses on and looked in the mirror, I honestly did not recognise myself! I looked behind me and wondered who it was in the mirror. It was me, this sort of skinny-looking thing. It really was, I was absolutely shattered.

I am not sure exactly how long we were there – three weeks or so I think – and all the men who had been captured in that part of northern France had passed through the camp on their way to Poland.

All the men who were desperately ill had been sent off to hospitals in Koblenz, a proper German hospital, so that our camp *lazarette* – that was the German word for a first aid post, was closed down.

They put us in a cattle truck to Poland. This was a proper cattle truck and because we were at the end of the mass of men passing through there were not too many people in the truck. We had just about enough room to lie down. It was a good thing we could lie down because we set off on a three-day journey to Poland.

PHASE FOUR

They threw a few loaves of bread in and closed the door and locked it. If you wanted to pee you did it in your boots. You stood up to reach a slit about 12 inches wide by 4 inches deep. You could just lean up and shove your shoe out and tip the pee out. It was a pretty drastic three days.

I was tall enough to be able to look out of this slit. So I know that we went through Magdeburg and on to Berlin. In Berlin I remember seeing Temple Hof Aerodrome. Just before the war, I had produced leaflets and advertising for Imperial Airways so I knew what it looked like.

We then went on to Poland. When the train drew in to the station, the sign said 'Thorn'.

PHASE FIVE

In July 1940, Thorn was be the HQ for Stalag XX-A. We were marched along the road and put into a huge hall, not surprising really, because we found out later that it was called 'The Balloon Hall'.

I presume it was a place where, in the 1914–18 war, they had kept balloons.

Thorn was on the River Vistula and the River Vistula was the front line between the Germans and the Russians pre-1914. The Germans had reinforced the town on the river and built a series of forts, almost underground, in a semi-circle around the town to protect it from attack by the Russians

Since 1919, it had been a Polish army headquarters. The German army was once again now in charge.

In the Balloon Hall we shuffled and were given a thin blanket each. There was straw all over the floor and we had to bunch it together to make it comfortable to lie on.

We always wore our uniform when we went to sleep.

We began to get into the routine of POW life.

As a clerk, I was called out to help with the business of registering everybody. Everybody had to give their name, army rank and number. They were then given a thin metal POW number. Mine was 12878. Photographs were taken of everyone. Religion, too, had to be given. Many of our men said, 'I am Jewish' so I put down 'C of E' because nobody wanted to admit that they were Jewish, not in Nazi Germany.

We were there a few days and then were sent on to Fort 12, one of the forts that I mentioned earlier. We were inside the fort; the German guards

PHASE FIVE

were outside the fort. Within the fort, we were free to wander around and see what was going on.

Only we were so hungry. But WERE we hungry!

Our daily ration was a bowl of soup at midday, a thick slice of bread at 4 o'clock, and first thing in the morning, a cup of coffee made from burnt barley or burnt acorns. That was all the food we had for the day. Some men were so starving that they would begin to queue at the cook house early in the morning. They hardly had the strength to stand up. They were just sitting or squatting; a great long queue of people waiting for the cook house to open at noon.

The bread ration

Most days we were issued with a loaf of bread between five men; very occasionally, it was restricted to one loaf between six.

Cutting up a loaf of bread equally between five watchful men is no mean task. 'Watchful' because every grain of bread really counts when it is all you have to eat each day apart from a scoopful of watery, tasteless soup. Everyone wanted the crust. The crust takes a bit of chewing and, therefore, was more desired.

By an extraordinary coincidence, it was discovered very early on, that a POW metal identity disc was one-fifth the size of a loaf. The POW number, which I still carry with me, is exactly 40mm wide. So 5 x 40mm = 200mm, the length of the loaf of bread they issued to us.

The loaf, called *Kommissbrot* – from the Kommissariat, the German Quartermaster's Store, was made from rye and had the date of baking stamped on the top. It was very wholesome bread and was on general issue to the German army.

If it was too new, it was too 'spongy' to cut. From our point of view, a fourteen-day old loaf was ideal. If it 'squeaked' as we cut it, it did not leave surplus crumbs.

In order to give as much 'crust' as possible to as many of the five people who shared the loaf, it had to be cut in a certain way. First, the person chosen to be the 'cutter' measured the loaf into five slices, using a POW metal plate. The centre piece was then carefully cut into a 40mm slice. The two pieces left were then cut in half, lengthways. By cutting the loaf this way, four 'end pieces' with two sides of crust were produced plus one 40mm slice of bread with the crust only around the edge.

Next came the draw for these pieces. It 'made your day' if you could 'win' a corner piece of bread. It was, almost, a tragedy to draw the 'slice' of bread.

So out came the cards. Aces high, cut. The five revealed their cards and the lowest card 'won' the slice – groan! The others picked up their 'corners' with a grin and rushed away to eat it with the bit of jam, made from flavoured swede, or margarine – synthetically made, but never the two at the same time.

The reason why the bread had to be eaten immediately was the utter impossibility of saving it. Where on earth could you keep it to stop it being stolen? Putting it in a pocket to save meant a pocketful of crumbs. Better to eat it immediately and avoid the disappointment of loss. If you exchanged something for a loaf of bread, which the men who went out on working parties and had contact with Polish civilians could do, then it was best to share it with one's mates immediately.

Some people, foolishly, would go to sleep lying on their loaf of bread only to discover, in the morning, that both ends had been cut off.

Usually when soldiers get together the conversation is sex. I promise you there was no sex talk here. We did not have the strength. All we talked about was food. Food. Food. Food. No other topic of conversation. We did not have any work and we just sat around thinking about food.

What have you done?

And then another strange happening. Somebody came round the fort to where we were all sitting on the ground, it was still summer, and said, 'Anybody here called Markham?'

So I said, 'Yes, that's me.'

And he said, 'Well they want you downstairs, then, in the office.'

In the office was a British sergeant major and he said, 'What have you been up to – the Germans want you?'

I said, 'I haven't been doing anything.'

'Honestly?'

I said, 'Well, I did have my prisoner of war number stolen the day before yesterday and reported it.'

So he said, 'Well, I don't think it's that. But anyway, you have got to have an interpreter to go with you and you have got to go to the German commandant.'

'What have you done?' I was shit scared.

PHASE FIVE

When I saw the German commandant, a very smartly dressed lieutenant with polished boots, etc., he said to me through the interpreter, 'What have you done? Because they want you at Stalag.'

By this time I was just about wetting my trousers.

We had two guards given to us and off we went.

The interpreter was called Eames. He moaned like the clappers.

'What have you done? You've got me involved with you. 'What trouble have you been in?'

And I said, 'I haven't been in any trouble. Honest.'

We eventually arrived at Stalag, this is short for Stammlager, Men's Camp. Stalag is headquarters for the whole of the area. We were in Stalag XX-A. That was because we were in the area covered by the 20th Germany Army. We reported to this headquarters, Eames, myself and the two guards.

There we met the Hauptman (captain), a huge, terrible-looking bloke. In fact, he was very friendly.

He said to me, 'You're Markham?'

'Yes Sir!'

'You are a *sanitater*?'

So the interpreter said to me, 'He says you're a shithouse waller.'

I said, 'No he didn't. He used the word *sanitater*, and in Germany that means medical orderly. You tell him, Yes, I am a medical orderly.'

The Hauptman said, 'Oh good. You are to go to Danzig to be the medical orderly on a working party. You will get a new uniform over there,' and pointed to a room.

'New boots over there.'

'New blankets over there.'

And I said, 'I've lost my prisoner of war number, Sir.'

'Oh. You get a new one from over there.'

He said to the interpreter, 'Be ready to move off in an hour.'

What was strange was that the Germans had obviously sent my name forward from Trier to Thorn. They had recognised that I had done a shitty job, quite well, and they were now going to send me, as a medical orderly, on a working party to Danzig.

That made a turning point in my life.

So in August 1940 off we went to Danzig. Danzig is a large town on the Baltic, called Gdanzk today. Off we went to the station and travelled, comfortably, in proper railway carriages. Two guards, me and my interpreter.

NO ESCAPE: THE MEMOIRS OF A POW IN STALAG XXA

I joined a working party at Danzig Oliva whose task was to construct the groundwork for a huge officers' training camp, which was to be built on the site.

This meant taking the top off a hill and pushing it down into the valley. In the valley it would make what the Germans called a *platz*, but what we would call the parade ground.

Our camp was, in those days, just a tent in a field surrounded by barbed wire, with a trench around it for drainage, where we lived and slept. There was a wooden hut where the German guards slept and a wooden hut where the cook house was.

One group of men within the camp started to construct huts for the rest of us for the winter; as it was summer it did not do us any harm to sleep in tents. There was just straw on the floor and we were very lousy and there was no way to delouse ourselves or have baths or anything at that time.

There were 200 men in the camp. A British sergeant major was in charge and I was the only medical orderly. Because it was a working party, the men had double rations, so we were adequately fed. Therefore, the health of these 200 wasn't too bad at all.

If anybody was very ill I could take them into town where there were some British soldiers of the Sherwood Forester Regiment, captured in Norway, who were well settled in. I could use their facilities to get my patient into hospital if I needed to do so. It was a good job they had such a facility because I did need to do so.

The men were working on top of the hill and pouring earth down, through wooden shutes, into the valley below. One day a man slipped and slid all the way down one of these shutes and broke his leg very badly. I rushed out from camp to find that he had a compound fracture. The bone was sticking through the flesh, which is a desperately dangerous thing.

I carefully strapped his leg up without getting the bone back underneath the flesh again, because that is unwise. It must be done under antiseptic conditions in a hospital. I then arranged for him to be sent off to hospital.

When I look back on the things I tackled without any training, I cringe! All I was, was just a Scout with a first aid badge!

In the camp, I used to hold medical parades in the morning to see if there were any men who were too sick to go to work. Usually there were a

PHASE FIVE

handful of men whom I did not want to go to work. The Germans did not argue. They took my word for it. In the evening, when they came back from work, I did another medical parade.

I got bandages and ointments and pills from the Germans. Once a week, a German medical orderly would come out to see how I was getting on and to give me equipment.

A horror story

A 'country' lad, came to see me one evening and said he had got a sore ankle. Looking at it I could see a huge abscess and I thought I saw the blue of the edge of another one.

I told him to take his trousers off. From ankle to hip his leg was covered in the most gruesome sores. Because we were lying on straw, the straw had got matted into these sores together with lice and the pus. It was an obnoxious sight.

I was so cross with him for letting himself go in that way. It was just sheer ignorance on his part. He could have come to me days before and got it sorted out.

So I went down to the cook house, got a scrubbing brush – one which they used to scrub the floor – got some hot water and I scrubbed every one of those ulcers until they bled.

He did not utter a word.

When I got them all fresh and clean I put Ichthyol (fish oil) ointment on them. Because the conditions we were living in were not too bad – decent food and everything – and the weather was beautiful, within ten days his legs were healed.

A fortnight later he was just a bad again, he had just let himself go again. It made me want to spit!

We begin to get organised – for a time!

As our camp was on a hill we had a view right across Danzig and the harbour. In the harbour was a German battleship, the *Admiral Speer*, a pocket battleship. The great harbour swept out to sea into the Baltic. Right in the distance we could see Gdynia.

It was a truly wonderful site for a camp and, because we were a working party, the Germans were very good to us. Just nearby was the popular seaside holiday resort of Zoppot. They used to take us swimming in the Baltic.

I could go down to the chemist and buy medicaments. Once a week I would take men down town to where the Sherwood Foresters were based. It meant that I had a good opportunity of looking round Danzig, which is a beautiful city.

We had sing-songs at night.

One of the most impressive moments of the week was on a Sunday when we would gather on a grassy bank, overlooking Danzig harbour, and hold a church service. One of our members had been a lay preacher and he led a very simple service. We sang 'Oh God our help in ages past …' and other hymns that we could remember – I still weep when we sing that in church. The whole camp turned up to hear very simple words from a very nice chap.

I must admit that out in the open, in the sun, with the glorious view, and after the trauma of being taken POW with the death and mayhem that we had gone through earlier, one really felt close to God. Christianity is a religion of the oppressed and we were certainly oppressed. We were a long way from home. We had had a pretty traumatic experience and we turned to God in our time of need.

I think it is worth recounting at this point that when we went back finally to Stalag the same kind of service used to take place every Sunday with the Hall absolutely packed solid with men. A very fine lay preacher would preach each Sunday. It was always a very moving service.

After about a year, the authorities managed to get this organised and sent out an official padre from Oflag. In the British army, ministers of religion are officers and gentlemen and are kept apart from the 'other ranks'. When chaplains were captured they were sent to Oflag.

So, as I say, about a year after we had been captured, things got organised and they sent out one of these official padres. He moved into a situation where every week the church had been full to capacity and it was a marvellous and wonderful experience. However, I think it took him just three weeks to finish up with him and the bloke who swept the floor. He cleared the whole lot of us out with his pious pedantry. Organised religion makes me sick!

Our ideal situation in Danzig ended in September when a new intake of 200 men came up from Stalag. The idea the Germans had was to double our workforce in order to speed up the work being carried out.

PHASE FIVE

The men who came were Scotsmen, from the Gorbals, the slums of Glasgow. They were little, short, stocky, runty fellows and they were sick, by God they were sick.

Members of the 51st Highland Division, they had been captured at St Valery and had had a terrible journey across Holland. They had been locked into the holds of a barge and left with the stench and filth and the heat. By the time they got to Danzig Oliva, none of them was ready for work.

The next morning was a shambles. The whole 200 fell out sick.

First, let me explain the hierarchical structure in the camp.

We had a British sergeant major who had been sent out from the NCO's camp to act as the man in charge of the British section. He was weak and ineffective, but some often were, they were office clerks and not military men, and this was a real office clerk, a weak weed.

On the German side, although there was a German officer somewhere around, the man who was really in command was an Unteroffizier.

Now an Unteroffizier is, theoretically, a corporal, but in the German army they are much better trained than the British army and have much more authority.

This German Unteroffizier was a super chap. He ran the camp very well indeed with this weak British sergeant major to help him. He and I got on very well and out of my original 200 men he would let the sick fall out each day – usually from 10–15 men.

This awful morning, we were faced with 200 genuinely sick guys. If they had been in the British army they would all have been in hospital. But they were not in the British army. They were prisoners of war and they were here to work. They had all volunteered to come on a working party. The reason they had volunteered was because they knew they were going to get double rations, whereas back in Stalag they were getting a very thin watery food.

So my usual 10 fell out plus 200 Scotties.

The German NCO looked at this lot with stark astonishment and turned to me and said, 'I've got twice the men, I've got to get twice the work from the working party. I can't have 200 men off sick, I'll tell you what I'll do, I'll let you have an extra 20.'

How could I choose 20, straight off the top of my head from the 200?

He said, 'Well, if you can't, I can.'

So he proceeded to count the first twenty men and said, 'Right you stay behind sick, the rest of you go to work.'

I said, 'Hold it, hold it. Stop.'

And I turned to the British sergeant major and said, 'Come on, help me out, I can't do this.'

'Well, you'll have to do it if the German NCO tells you to,' said the British sergeant major. 'What a twit,' I thought.

Just imagine the situation. Faced with 200 sick men I had to choose 20, who were the sickest, to stay behind, whilst the rest went on to the working party.

True they probably would not have worked very hard. But, nevertheless, they had to go out and spend the day out in the field somewhere giving the impression of doing work.

I lined them up, so it was easier to do and inspection. 'What's wrong with you?'

'Sore head.'

'You can go to work. What's wrong with you?'

'Sore head.'

'You can go to work. What's wrong with you?'

'Sore stomach.'

'You can go to work. What's wrong with you?'

'I've got this great ulcer on my leg.'

'You stand over there. I'll have a look later at you.' And so I went on down the whole line.

But then came the crunch point. As I proceeded down the line, one of these Scotties fainted.

Very impressive.

Collapsed and fell on the floor.

And that was that.

When I got to him, I stepped over him and said, 'And he can go to work.' And on I went.

When I had finished I had got thirty men and I said to the German, 'There we are, there's thirty men who've got to stay behind.'

And he said, 'Well what about that one,' and pointed to the chap who had fainted.

So I went up to him, kicked him and said, 'Go on, go to work.'

He got up and said, 'You rotten bastard,' and off he went. He was making it up. I can tell you, I was glad he did get up. Because if I had made a mistake I would have had egg all over my face. I had sized him up as one of those types of lads who puts it on. That was a big moment in my life. I made the decision that he was faking. That he was not really sick. I was on my own in making the decision. There was nobody backing me, nobody supporting me. It was a pretty scary feeling at the time. Have faith!

Another medical story.

Late one evening I was in the surgery, on my own, and a sergeant came in complaining of violent stomach pains. He was not a military sergeant – he was a clerk in the Intelligence Corps. A very intelligent, very nice lad. But not a tough guy. He was a school teacher, not a soldier. But he was doubled up with pain. What on earth do you do in a situation like that?

There was no way that I could get him down to the hospital at that time of night and frankly my medical knowledge was not all that great – not at that time. However, I had a shrewd feeling that he was putting it on a bit, he wanted sympathy.

So I talked to him. He got a pain every now and then. So I thought it was worthwhile trying one of my psychological things.

I am a great believer in faith healing – I believe that you can heal yourself better than using medicines – so I got a tablet which I said was very strong. I gave it a great build-up. I said I was given it by a German orderly that morning. He guaranteed that it was very good at curing stomach ache.

As a matter of fact, it was valerian, which is a herb from way, way back that you can use to soothe stomach cramps. So it was not all 'bull'.

I gave him this tablet and said, 'You've got to be patient. It takes about forty-five seconds for it to work.'

We sat there and counted the forty-five seconds. The pain had gone.

Oh well – Faith is a marvellous thing.

A British doctor arrives

After about another month, another change took place. Because they were getting the camp sorted out and were getting the wooden huts built, we were getting some semblance of organisation, not just sleeping under canvas.

So they sent a British doctor out from Oflag. This, of course, was a tremendous relief for me. He was a nice chap called Knowles. Funnily enough, his father was a printer and did work for me in the advertising agency before and after the war. It was quite interesting. By that time also there was another chap called Rimmer who was also acting as a medical orderly. We had a very enjoyable time with Dr Knowles. He taught us a great deal.

He talked a lot about childbirth and menstrual periods and fertile time information which came in very handy after the war when Trudy, my wife, and I already had our son, Michael, and wanted to have Wendy and Timothy at special times – and it worked!

Another thing Dr Knowles taught us was how to play bridge. We got a foursome and we played bridge, bridge, bridge, bridge and bridge. It was super.

We got three good meals a day. The conditions in which we were sleeping were excellent. We had good bedding in bunk beds which were warm and dry. We had shower baths.

Danzig itself was super.

But all good things come to an end and when it was coming up to winter they decided that there was no point in working over the winter and they would send us all back to Stalag.

So this wonderful, ideal situation all came to a close. We got on a train and went back to Stalag. What an awful business.

News from Foots Cray

My mum and dad heard from the Royal Artillery Records Office in Foots Cray, Sidcup, Kent, on 14 August, that I was a POW, and on 5 October the address they could send letters to. I received my first letter from Dad in the first week of November. It was a great strain for them to have to wait from May until August to get official confirmation that I was a POW. It was also an enormous relief to me to hear from them. I had known that I was alright. I was, therefore, very glad to know that they were alright and that they knew I was alright.

PHASE SIX

In November 1940, we were sent to Camp 13A. That first night we were shepherded into the black hut. Imagine a barn about 40ft high, 200ft long and 100ft wide, with a concrete floor, black as pitch, because there were only two or three low wattage lamps in the whole of this hut. Winter in Germany starts in October and goes through to March. The hut was filled with three-tier bunks. The top bunk was level with my eyes. The bottom bunk touching the floor.

It was freezing cold and black and we were told to sleep on the bottom bunks because everybody else had taken the best bunks. The lower you are the colder it is and later that winter men on the bottom bunks froze to death overnight.

We did not freeze to death in November, but it was jolly cold. It was black, it stank and it was filthy. The straw we had to lie on was crawling with lice. What a contrast to Danzig.

Appel

Every morning and evening the Germans counted us. They called the parade 'Appel' and would shout 'Raus, Raus, Los, Los' at us to try to speed us on to parade.

We always had to line up in fives for them to count us. Germans can only count in fives – 5, 10, 15, 20 and so on. They never ever did it right. It took hours, standing in the freezing cold, until, eventually, they satisfied themselves that 'Alles' was in 'Ordnung' to let us rush back to the huts.

Then began my first winter away from home. It was one of the most dreadful times of all.

I must admit, that me being me, it took me about a week to get onto the top bunk. You can always find a way if you want to. But it was still very grim.

I was a medical orderly and as they did not have medical work for me to do, I did not have to work. So, although most of the men went out on working parties, I did not have to go, which was a godsend.

Out boots had worn away and we were given wooden Dutch clogs with rags wrapped around our feet, which were very uncomfortable. All night long you would hear the click, clack, click, clack as men went outside to pee. You had to go out across the snow, across the platz to the loos; it froze as soon as you peed.

If you were to leave some of your coffee to drink later it would freeze overnight. If you dropped coffee on the floor it would freeze from November to March. When winter really started the awfulness of it overtook us.

The temperature fell to -30° C. It was so cold that, one day, on parade I opened my eyes wide and found, to my horror that the tears in my eyes were freezing.

This big hut had a wooden roof and it leaked all along the slats of the roof. The whole roof was covered in stalactites of ice. As water dripped through the roof and froze, it became an icicle, more dripping, more freezing became a bigger icicle so that by Xmas the roof was covered in 2ft-long icicles.

The windows too were thick with ice.

We received a cup of coffee first thing, which was not coffee, it was 'ersatz', i.e. burnt acorns which had been crushed and brewed up. Horrid stuff even with a bit of sugar in it.

That was breakfast.

At lunchtime we had a very watery soup.

At teatime we had a slice of bread about 1¼in thick. Sometimes we had a bit of margarine, sometimes a bit of jam and then nothing until breakfast the next morning – which was a cup of coffee. That was the daily routine: coffee, watery soup made of swede and barley, and a chunk of bread. It was horrid. It came to fewer than 1,000 calories, so it was real starvation diet.

PHASE SIX

The soup ration

In the cookhouse they had two big boilers in which to make the soup. They put in all the vegetables, the rotten potatoes and swedes and barley and a bit of fat. Then the cooks (British) would boil it up.

There was a settlement so that the top of the soup was very watery and the bottom very thick. To overcome this and make it a bit more equal they had a man with a wooden paddle whose job it was to stir it up so that it became the same consistency throughout.

But he was an idle bloke and he did not work very hard with the result that whatever happened the top of the boiler was always thin soup, the bottom of the boiler was always thick soup.

So the trick was to get into line, to make sure you got thick soup because if you got thick soup it made your day. If you got the thin soup you were really starving for the rest of the day.

However, there were some men that were so hungry they could not resist. They had to queue up. They had to be first into the cookhouse.

OK, so everybody else stood back.

The snag was that those in the know all stood back and then there was a surge forward as everybody moved to get in the queue that they hoped they would get the bottom of the first boiler.

If you really made a right mess of it, instead of getting the bottom of the first boiler and all the good thick soup, the cooks would shut that boiler off and you would get the top of the next boiler.

You got thin soup.

I know it sounds silly but, under those conditions, whether you had a thick soup or a thin soup meant whether you were starving or just desperately starving.

Mail from home

We were given 'letter forms' which we had to use in order to write home. In return we received letters from home.

Dad wrote to me every week as regular as clockwork and I wrote home whenever I was given a letter form.

On average, Dad's letters to me took about ten days though on one momentous occasion it only took seven days. Home seemed so close that week. He handed my letters over to the local *Willesden Chronicle*.

Reading now the extracts that the paper published, I see that my letters home did not reveal the depths to which we had sunk. I realise that I did not want to worry them too much. There was absolutely no point in painting the true picture. They could not do anything about it, so I tried to keep 'their tails up'. On reflection, all these years later, I am sure that I was right to 'Gild the lily'.

Xmas 1940

It was coming up to my first Christmas away from home. The previous year in October had been my twenty-first birthday. Grandma had given me a wristwatch and, unbelievably, I still had it – I did not smoke and therefore there was no need for me to hock it for cigarettes. Also, the Germans who had captured us had been very correct and did not pinch our watches – which was unusual. I must admit that I was one of the few people in the Camp 13 with a watch.

We were covered in lice, we were filthy, we stank, we were cold, the straw we slept on was literally crawling with lice and we were starving. We were in a terrible, terrible state. I suppose at that time we were as bad as the pictures you see of the Belsen people. We had men who were so skinny that instead of having bottoms they had a recess into the pelvis. It was awful, really awful.

Amongst all this squalor and frightfulness and awfulness, in this black hut with its icy stalactites, I had my Rotary watch. At Christmas I unscrewed the back and there was this beautiful piece of mechanism, little ruby jewels glistening and the movement going on in such a disciplined way, tick-tock, tick-tocking away reminding me of Grandma and Mum, Dad, Mabel and Doug.

Oh what a moment. I cried.

The Lice

Lice are like little ants. They suck your blood, they spread typhus, and they are disastrous. They bite you. They crawl all over you and you can never ever, for one moment, not feel them crawling, night and day, night and day. You cannot get rid of them.

PHASE SIX

The reason you cannot get rid of them is because of the intense cold – you cannot strip off. You cannot take your clothes off because it is freezing. You have to sit in your overcoats, even inside the building.

So to delouse you had to take your overcoat off and shiver. You would look under the collar – under the seam– to find these little ant-like lice and crack them between the two thumb nails. They go crack and squelch and it squashes blood over your thumb nails.

You keep on doing this, as you might have thirty or forty along the collar of your overcoat alone, then you take your jacket off and put your overcoat on and try and do that with your trousers. So that might, if you were lucky, kill another 100 lice. All to no avail. As soon as you lay down on the straw again, you were crawling.

What was extraordinary about these lice was that they seemed to get into the pores of the skin.

Later on, much later on when I was working in the hospital, we would have men in. We would strip them, burn their clothes, give them a bath and put them in clean pyjamas and into bed. Within an hour they were lousy again.

The lice would, literally, breed from the pores of the skin. You had to bath a man every day for a week and keep giving him changes of pyjamas before, ultimately, you managed to get him clean.

In January I got a Red Cross parcel from Dad. Dad had been a soldier in the First World War. He knew how awful it was in the trenches and how cold it was and therefore, God bless him, he thought of me out there in the cold and he sent me woollen underpants – long johns and a woollen vest with long sleeves. As it was, he only sent one pair. I assumed that he could only send one pair because he had to sacrifice clothing coupons to get these woollies for me. So it was a great sacrifice for parents to send clothing.

But to me they were useless. What was the point in the middle of winter of putting on long johns and a vest when, within minutes, they would be crawling with lice in all this wool. I would not have been able to live with it. It was just terrible.

I could never use them because I could never wash them. If I washed them, I could never get them dry – they would just freeze.

You cannot imagine how bad it was.

I thought, 'there is only one thing I can do. There is no point in my wearing them and destroying them. If I sell them I might get something useful for them.' So I did.

I got bread which filled my belly for two or three days. I also got a bottle of Schnapps. At Christmas I drank it. All in one evening. The whole bottle, myself, and I did not care.

I understand why people get drunk under those kind of conditions. It's oblivion. You feel happy and warm and the whole world seems wonderful and you go off into a deep sleep and you do not feel the lice and you do not feel the cold and it is absolutely wonderful.

I woke up the next morning, I had been violently sick in the night and I felt fabulous. I did not have a hangover. I felt uplifted. In fact my morale was high and I felt absolutely super. I felt like facing the day.

That was one of the two times in my life that I had been drunk. The other time was twenty years later with a client who had just been told that his wife was dying of cancer. He drank a bottle of gin and I drank a bottle of whisky to keep him company.

Under POW conditions you get drunk when you can. It was a soporific effect. There is no question that Dad's bottle of Schnapps certainly did me the power of good that Christmas. I am sure it did a lot more good than a pair of long johns would have done.

One quite amusing story.

I managed somehow to get a Polish hat, a civilian hat, which I wore. It was the only Polish civilian hat in the camp. One evening, I was asked by the sergeant major if I would give it up.

It was explained that it was for an escaping officer. It was for Airey Neave (Margaret Thatcher's right-hand man whose car, with him in it, was blown up by the IRA at the House of Commons), who had managed to get to our camp.

In his book, which I had and lost, he talks about Camp 13 and about making a break from the dentist. He had my Polish civilian hat as part of his disguise.

The camp was surrounded by barbed wire and on the other side of the barbed wire there were the forests and you could hear the wolves howling.

PHASE SIX

The water tank froze. You could not wash. You could not keep yourself clean and you were hungry.

The only good thing we did have in the camp was a library. And what a godsend that was to me. In forty days I read forty detective stories. I have not read a detective story since. I cannot bear them, but at the time it was a great relief for me to be able to do that to take my mind off the awfulness around us.

A Newspaper!

Amazing though it may seem, the Germans who were sure that they had won the war, took time to try to indoctrinate us into the Nazi way of life. They appointed a *Sonderfuhrer*, a special leader, whose task it was to 'turn' us to Nazism! He spoke good English and tried to ingratiate himself with us.

To help him, the German authorities produced a newspaper which they called *The Camp*. It was filled with news from England.

Let's face it, the news from home at that time was pretty grim. All they had to do was to report the facts. They quoted quite widely from someone, who I had never heard before, called Aneurin Bevan. He seems to spend most of his time in the House of Commons criticising Mr Churchill. It made very despondent reading in a prison camp in Poland.

They continued with the newspaper for a year or so, but the *Sonderfuhrer* was returned to wherever they breed '*Sonderfuhrers*'.

I volunteered to go on a working party for a very short time when they started a laundry. I thought it was a worthwhile job going to help. At least it was warm and I worked for a week in this laundry trying to get clothes clean. At least it meant that MY clothes were clean. Unfortunately, in that kind of situation, survival is the name of the game. You do not have the time to care about anybody else because if you do, you die. We lost a lot of men that first winter.

We used to bait the Goons; the Goons was the name we gave to the German guards. One of the things we would do was to collect lice and instead of killing them we would put them in a jar. As the Goons came round at Appel, counting, you would tip the lice over their jackets.

That was always good for a laugh, but if you were caught you went to the bunker.

Bunkah! Bunkah! Bunkah! That is what the Germans used to call it. You were put in an empty, cold room in the German guardhouse for a time. If it was a serious crime – fortunately, we did not have any serious crimes – then you would be sent away to a proper punishment (Straff) prison.

PHASE SEVEN

In February 1941, I was taken out of this dreadful Camp 13A and sent about a quarter of a mile up the road to Fort 13. Lice and filth were a major health hazard and it was sensible to send me, a spare medical orderly, up to this fort to help operate the old Polish army delouser. That is what I did.

The bath house was in two sections. The first section had the delouser. The second was the bath house proper.

My function was to operate the delouser. It was a brick-built box about 4ft 6in high, about 3ft wide and about 8ft long, basically, just a hot room. There was a space underneath where you lit a big fire to get this thing as hot as possible. It had a door at each end. I put the dirty clothes in one end on hangers and cooked them for half an hour, which theoretically killed all the lice. They were taken out at the other end and given to the men who, by then, had passed through the bath house and were clean. I was the custodian of the fire and water pump and it was my job to keep the fire going and pump water into the bath house. Each evening I could put my clothes through the hot room, go round to the clean side and have a good bath. So that, for the first time in months, I was lice free.

The fire and water pump were two very valuable assets in these conditions. It was the only water source in the Fort. It was also the only fire where people could cook their odds and ends. They made cakes out of broken biscuits and used to push them into the delouser to cook. They did not mind if a few lice fell on them.

One of the snags of being in the public eye like that was that, as my watch had not been stolen (it was one of about four watches in the whole of this 2,000-man camp), I had to tell the time to everybody walking up and down the corridor in the Fort all day long.

I have pictures of the entrance to the Fort. Fort 15 was very similar except that the moat was cultivated by us as a vegetable garden. You can see it has a deep dry moat around it. It was built before 1913 by the Germans when Thorn was on the border between Germany and Russia. What they had done was to put grass all over the top and in the forty or fifty years since it was built, trees had also grown. The result was the top of the Fort was just like the country. We, literally, had country walks around the top of the Fort. From the top there were views right across the countryside. It was, in fact, a quite nice place to be held as a POW.

The Germans had their 'Salisbury Plain' there. We could see their artillery practising. They were also developing rocket launchers with about twelve rockets together. They would fire them all at once. What a noise as they took off.

By the side of one of the forts was a railway. We could see the trains taking the German army off to the Russian front. Later those trains brought the wounded back from the front.

We had a concert party in the Fort and I saw some of the shows that they put on: the play *It Pays to Advertise*, which was well produced and acted, and *Happy Days*. Both were regularly produced at Fort 13.

Trumpeter

This large, efficiently run Fort, had a trumpeter: 'Get out of bed, get out of bed, you lazy —', for the morning and a wonderful 'Last Post' at night.

One day, General Beck, the chief of the 20th German Army, whose control we were under, came visiting. Resplendent in medal bedecked uniform with his red tabs and red stripe down the sides of his trousers, the general began his inspection of the Fort by walking across the roadway, crossing the dry moat. The trumpeter stepped forward and played the tune *Colonel Bogey*.

Now this tune, a very imposing march, has very, very rude words sung to it in America, where the tune came from, and the British army. The German general, not recognising the tune for what it was, but thinking that it was the British 'general salute' came to a halt, in the middle of the bridge and gave a very smart salute. The top of the Fort was lined with our men who had the greatest trouble restraining their hysterical, silent, laughter!!

Because we were inside this huge brick building it was quite warm unlike the black hut at Camp 13A where it really was desperately cold. Because I had an interesting job at the bath house, I could keep clean all the time, and, because I could offer favours, like using the oven fire and the water pump, I could get little extras.

I suppose you could say we were getting ourselves organised to POW life. The men in the camp went out in working parties, with twenty or thirty men at a time going out with a German guard. They would go somewhere in Thorn and clear out a storeroom or work on a plot of land or just do odd unskilled labouring jobs.

Going to the dentist

At the Fort we had a dentist and a doctor. I had been at the Fort over a year and was at the hospital Fort 14 when I needed to go to the dentist. I asked around and discovered that a small party of half a dozen had to be made up to arrange an appointment at the dentist in Fort 13. As I was a senior medic, I was given the task of finding six people in Fort 14 who needed to go to the dentist.

I booked an afternoon, a week ahead, and soon found my six – five plus me. On the day, I went round Fort 14 getting them into a party to go to the dentist at Fort 13, but, surprise, surprise, they ALL had very urgent reasons why they could not go THAT particular afternoon. So I went on my own.

When I arrived at Fort 13, the dentist, a charming New Zealand lieutenant, said, 'I have written off the whole of the afternoon for a party from Fort 14 so you had better make yourself comfortable because you are going to be here for the afternoon. And so it was.

He must have done ten fillings in my teeth. True, they needed the treatment – but ten fillings! He used a very old-fashioned treadle machine to operate the drill! I was exhausted.

On reflection, it was probably a blessing in disguise. By doing all my bad teeth at one go he set me up until I returned home when our local dentist in London, where I lived, did them all again – but NOT in one afternoon.

How we pinched the bread

There was a bread storeroom in the Fort which a German looked after. Once a day, he came in to hand out the ration of bread. The bread was counted as it went into the storeroom and if we were to steal it we had to steal it BEFORE it got to the storeroom.

The water pump I controlled was the only water in the Fort so the cook house had to draw its water from this pump which was 100 yards away. Four men carried what can only be described as half a barrel with two long slats of wood, like a stretcher, nailed to either side. These four men would bring the empty barrel along, fill it up with water and cart it back to the cook house. It was quite a hefty job and they would do this three or four times a day.

On the days when the Germans had the bread delivered to the bread store in the Fort, they kept a lorry outside the Fort. Men were lined up and had to carry five loaves at a time from the lorry to the bread store. What happened on one extraordinary day was that the chaps who normally carried water for the cook house carried a completely empty barrel. As the men with the bread walked past them they tipped their five loaves of bread into the dry half barrel until it was full of bread. The men then lifted the barrel up high, put it on their shoulders and walked past the Germans with a barrel load of bread, which we all shared out afterwards. The Germans never did discover how we stole so much bread.

My sojourn in Fort 13 was not very long – from February 1941 to May 1941. I was told to see the senior British Officer, who in fact was a doctor, who said I was to go to Fort 14.

PHASE EIGHT

May 1941. Fort 14 was the hospital and had a proper moat round it filled with water. It was quite a small fort and had been used as the Polish army hospital for the area, staffed with Polish doctors. When the British POWs were sent to the Fort it was still staffed with Polish doctors and Polish medical orderlies. These were to be sent to Polish POW camps and the Fort was being restructured. British medical orderlies and British doctors were being put in charge. By the time I arrived there were no Poles at all, it was all British run.

Three of us were sent from Fort 13. We were lined up in front of a Royal Army Medical Corps regimental sergeant major. He looked at us all and said that we looked pretty hopeless. He assigned Ron Dryden and myself to be cleaners of the lavatory, in other words we were 'shithouse wallahs'. Our first task was to clean out the shithouses.

The Fort itself was a small brick fort and above, where there were grass and lawns, the Germans had built wooden barracks. At the end of each barracks were the lavatories. Four little cubicles with wooden seats with wooden buckets underneath. Each day these wooden buckets, which were full of shit, had to be collected, carried down to the brick building and tipped into a cess-pool which was adjacent to the proper brick-built lavatories in the Fort itself. There was a metal cover to the cell-pool. Ron and I had to lift off the cover and tip the contents of the wooden buckets into the cess-pool.

Once a month, a Pole would come along with a horse and a tank-like vehicle. He would scoop out the shit and put it into the tank. He would then take it away to spread on the fields.

Then Ron and I had to clean up the lavatories. We were given chloride of lime. It sterilised and whitened all the woodwork. So this was our job.

Each day we would take each of the loos in turn, carry the bucket full of shit, which the patients had been using all night, and empty it in the cesspool, go back again and again until all four loos had been emptied. It sounds a filthy job – it was a filthy job – but Ron and I made a joke of it.

This is what we did. We commandeered, from all sorts of sources, a uniform. We each got ourselves a blue Chasseau D'Alpine overcoat from the storeroom; we got jeans, or rather cotton trousers, boots and berets, which we put feathers in. We had our brooms and would march around the Fort very much like Walt Disney's Dwarfs (Hi ho, Hi ho, it's off to work we go...) it was quite a joke. In fact, it was such a joke that when later I ran a Christmas pantomime, with a fancy-dress party, two fellows went as us. We were a real comic turn and we had the last laugh.

We worked rapidly. We did not mooch about. We were finished by lunchtime, so we could go down to the bath house, put our dirty clothes on the hangers, go through the bath house and put on our brand-new uniforms and spend the rest of the afternoon enjoying ourselves while everybody else was working. No question at all – Ron and I had the last laugh.

An even bigger laugh – the funniest thing of all, really – was that because we did the job so well, because the loos were so brilliantly white, the Germans noticed us and the British medical officers noticed us. We came to the attention of all and sundry to such a degree that we were told to stop being shithouse wallahs and become medical orderlies. So Ron and I were drafted to the surgical side of the Fort.

There were four wooden huts on the top of the fort called 'Barracks': one for surgical cases, one for the 'infectious' cases and another two for medical cases.

The surgical ward wooden barracks were quite long with two very large rooms, one at each end, each big enough for about twenty-four men with two RAMC medical orderlies in charge. In one end were Ron Dryden and Bill Brickell. At my end were me and Harry Morice. The centre third was split into three rooms: an operating theatre; a room with half a dozen beds, enough for the Intensive Care Unit (another medical orderly, Bill Foster, was in charge of that); and then a room which was the quarters for two doctors.

PHASE EIGHT

Now what was interesting was that Harry Morice was not a medical orderly at all. Harry was the British Commandant of the Fort. The word the Germans used was *Vertrauensmann*, the British 'The man of confidence', the chap that liaised between us and the Germans. He looked after all the food distribution, laundry and things like that.

The trouble was, that at that time, the Germans did not make allowances for that job. They only recognised medical orderlies, so the only place they could house Harry was with me in my section of the barrack. This meant that I ran the whole of my end of the barrack of twenty-four patients on my own.

Later when, finally, the Germans really did allow Harry to have his own room I had another medical orderly as an assistant. Funnily enough this was the Bombardier Jim Ward, who had been in charge of stretcher bearers in my own regiment. When he finally came to Thorn, I was in charge and he was MY assistant, because by that time, I had so much more experience.

Bedding

In the hospital, the beds, apart from the intensive care beds, were two-tier bunk beds. The lower bed was a normal bed. The upper bed was 1.3m high. The beds were made of wood, with plank sides and wooden slats to hold straw-filled paillasses.

German soldiers, in hospital or base camps, put their blankets into a blue-checked cover. We had been sent 'quilts' from Turkey so we fitted our quilts into these blue-checked covers. We had white sheets over the paillasses and blue-checked covers over the straw-filled pillows. Each week we changed the sheets and quilt covers and, through Harry, had them laundered. Permanent staff had extra Turkish quilts which we could fold into two and put over the straw paillasses for extra comfort.

Skin troubles

Under the conditions in which we lived in camp we had a wide range of skin disorders to treat, from crabs, scabies, ringworm up to the more horrendous ulcers and carbuncles – the latter we treated by cutting away the mass of rotted flesh, like a thick rotten steak.

We had a range of ointments and dyes to treat the various skin conditions we met. Often, we would treat massive leg ulcers by wrapping the leg with plaster of Paris and letting it 'stew' for a week or so.

I clearly remember being in surgery when we received a group of men from a working party who had lived under terrible conditions. I ripped off a dressing over an ulcer to find it covered in lice. I looked at my hand which held the dressing and it too was crawling with lice. I had been free of such horrors for a year. I flung the dressing into the stove to burn and washed and washed and washed my hands – eugh!

We had to build an operating theatre

We fitted it out, scrubbed it clean and one morning we started operating. The Germans supplied the equipment, instruments, etc., and to start with, the dressings and drugs. Later, the Red Cross sent us special parcels full of drugs and dressings. The German bandages were of white crepe paper with paper padding instead of cotton wool. The Red Cross material was of the normal top-quality cotton bandages, cotton wool, etc.

As a matter of fact, I preferred to use the German paper bandages because a) we threw them away after use, and b) the crepe paper moulded itself to the shape of the limb being bandaged. The British cotton bandages had to be saved, washed, rewound and used again.

We had two teams. We had two doctors and one doctor was responsible for each end of the barrack. Captain McMillan was a British army doctor, working with Ron Dryden and Bill Brickell, and I was working with Flying Officer Cullen, an RAF doctor who had been captured in Crete.

To start with, we just did brutal things – really crude ulcers and abscesses and boils with pus all over the place. It was all grim, bloody stuff. But we got our hand in and as long as you did not faint that was fine.

And then one day, the doctors called us all into their room in the evening and said, 'Tomorrow we are going to try a clean, sterile operation and this is how we will do it: Mr Cullen will do one operation and Mr McMillan will do the next one. While Mr Cullen is operating, Mr McMillan will give the anaesthetic and while Mr McMillan is operating Mr Cullen with give the anaesthetic.'

PHASE EIGHT

Mr McMillan had Billy Brickell as his assistant and Mr Cullen had me as his assistant. David Thomas, a RAMC sergeant was the sterile nurse who handled the instruments.

The first 'sterile' operation we did was for varicose veins. Mr Cullen had to tie-off the femoral vein high up in the thigh. It is a very simple thing to do when you know how, but it was our first attempt at a real sterile operation; we had to be very, very careful.

The previous evening, we had scrubbed the whole of the operating theatre from floor to ceiling. We really scrubbed everything and boiled all the instruments.

So that on the morning of the operation, Mr Cullen and I, who were operating first, scrubbed-up while Mr McMillan and Billy Brickell gave the anaesthetic. We all scrubbed and scrubbed – you have seen how they do it in hospitals. We just had a bowl of hot water. We did not have sterile gloves or anything so we really had to scrub clean.

I know now why they call it an operating theatre. The drama of curtain-up.

Let me describe the scene.

Outside it is prison camp, cold, dirty, lousy and smelly. Inside this room, it was warm, it was clean, it smelt heavily of ether – because that was the anaesthetic we were using, and there was a stillness, an ordered discipline, about everything. Then Mr Cullen looked round and said to Mr McMillan 'How is everything your end?'

'Fine.'

The patient was deeply asleep.

Mr Cullen looked at me.

'OK?'

'Yes.'

He looked at the sterile nurse and at the 'dirty' nurse, who had to pick up bits and pieces and mop everyone's brow and push Mr McMillan's glasses back off the end of his nose, or run errands or whatever was needed.

'Everybody ready,' and made the first incision.

There was blood oozing out as the scalpel cut across the chap's thigh. I swabbed.

Absolute pure drama. Every time it happened and it happened hundreds of times in the end, it was always drama to me. The poor fellow who was on the operating table had his neck on the block because we might have killed him, but, as a matter of fact, we did not kill anybody.

We did not lose a single man in that operating theatre and I think that was a marvellous effort.

After the operation, the man was put on a stretcher and carried back into the ward, where we waited until he came round.

The first few cases went into the intensive care unit where they were watched very carefully in case anything went septic. Fortunately, nothing did go septic.

You do not have such a thing as luck; we took great care, which is what it was. We went on and did other small operations for about a year. Twice a week we would have operations, once with one doctor, once with the other.

We would start the morning with a sterile operation such as varicose veins and then go on to circumcisions – we had lots of those in a prison camp – and then we would get on to haemorrhoids. Now that was a very bloody operation. We would put on rubber aprons and really get stuck in with a load of blood.

Finally, we would end the morning in style with septic things, with pus going all over the floor. So we started all nice and sterile and clean and finished with a gory mess, but it was very good fun. At least it was for us.

When we carried our haemorrhoids' operations we gave the patients a spinal anaesthetic, which was very tricky; it paralysed the lower part of their body for a time. Now the lower part of their body contains the bladder and the result was that some of these poor chaps were absolutely yelling with pain because their bladder was so distended. But because their muscles had paralysed, they could not pass water. So one of my tasks was to help them

Just picture this.

Late evening. Dark outside. A wooden hut with a single bulb in the middle of the room. Men were lying in two-tier bunk beds. We always put the chaps who were due to have the operation in the bottom bunk. The chap on the top had a straw mattress.

I had to pass a catheter, which means you push the catheter up the orifice in the man's penis, until it has gone into the bladder. The urine comes out and relieves the pressure.

This has to be a very, very sterile operation because otherwise you get germs into the bladder and then the man has real problems.

PHASE EIGHT

Can you imagine what it was like? With hardly any light, bending down under a bunk, with the straw dust coming down from above, trying to pass a catheter? The little pipe in the penis is very small and to try and force a plastic tube up there is no joke, particularly under those conditions.

With haemorrhoid cases we had to give enemas beforehand and lots of injections. We were fairly skilful by this time and we orderlies could give an injection better than the doctors. Giving injections was an extraordinary business.

Sometimes, because the men were in pain, we would give them morphia. The trouble was that some fellows would almost come to depend upon it and you would have an extraordinary situation. I have had men absolutely crying to be given morphia.

I have gone over and said, 'You know I can't give you morphia without the doctor's orders.'

'Oh Vic, please, please,' says the chap. 'You know you can get it from the surgery.'

In the end you would say, 'For goodness sake keep your mouth shut and don't let the doctor know that I have done this.'

So I would go into the surgery and fill the syringe with sterile water and return with this syringe already filled and say, 'If you let the doctor know I am giving you morphia, he'll have my guts for garters.'

'No Vic, no, no. Oh but please, please. Come on Vic, quick, quick'.

I said, 'I will just do it slow. Just feel it as it goes in. Now, there, it's going in, feel it?'

'Oh what a relief, Vic. Thank you ever so much. I won't breathe a word, honest, but oh, I was really on my beams end then. Thank you ever so much.'

So there would be this lad absolutely pain free from just distilled water.

Faith healing!

We did the small operations for about a year and then Mr Cullen had us in to his room one night. Mr Cullen was the senior surgeon of the two doctors. He said, 'Right we are going to take the next big step forward. We are going to try an appendix.'

Now that really was quite a big step.

And the other operation we did a few weeks later was a hernia. These were the two that we specialised in. Appendix and hernias. Mr Cullen would get all the books out and get a blackboard and he draw on it to show us exactly what was going to happen.

The next morning, when the operation was taking place, he would talk it all through and say, 'Look here's the muscle as I said,' and 'Look here we are separating it and not cutting across it.' And 'Look we cut through and this is where the appendix should be,' and 'God, where is it?'

It is not all that easy. Opening somebody up under our conditions, where we tried to keep the incision as small as possible because we did not want too much dirt and that going in, was a bit tricky.

You opened up his tummy and it was just bloody.

You think, 'which bloody bit is his gut and which bloody bit is his appendix?'

Sometimes it was a bit of a panic, particularly when the appendix was on the other side of the gut.

The patients, unfortunately, did not restrict themselves just to have need for hernias and appendix to suit us, they had all sorts of other things, peptic ulcers and everything.

One day a week we had an ambulance to take us to Thorn to the big hospital called, by the Germans, *Reserve Lazarett* Thorn.

We would go into the X-ray room; the Germans would move out and we would move in to operate the X-ray machines and equipment, take X-rays and then come to a diagnosis.

The hospital had a ward staffed by two British medical orderlies. If we wanted a really skilful operation carried out we could send up to twelve men into this ward in the big hospital to be treated.

Here is another of my 'funny' stories.

In June 1941, the Germans swept into Russia and their casualties were enormous. Thorn was the first hospital to which the Northern Army could send their men. In fact, German soldiers would come into Thorn hospital still wearing the field dressings that had been put on when they were injured. Some of them were in a terrible state with the original tourniquet still in place – which meant that what may have started as a simple wound was now gangrenous.

There were so many casualties that the German doctors did not have the time to play around with clever, clever treatment. The result was that if there was anything wrong with your arm, off it came. Anything wrong with your leg, off it came, with no argument. It was easier to heal an amputation

PHASE EIGHT

than go through the fiddle faddle of trying to repair wounds. It was sheer butchery and it was frightful, but that is what happened.

Now the odd bit is this. We had a man who had a desperately bad leg. We thought it was osteomyelitis and we sent him down with a recommendation for an amputation.

The German doctor said, 'Oh no, we will save his leg.' They worked on our British soldier for upwards of a year and in the end they saved his leg from being amputated. Whereas downstairs, in that same hospital, they were lopping off German soldiers' legs and arms as easy as 'kiss your hand'.

It was typical Nazi arrogance. They wanted to prove to us how superior they were.

We were one side of the Vistula and the hospital in the town, was on the other side. Sometimes we went to the hospital by ambulance. Sometimes we marched; we had to march across a railway bridge.

Later on, we saw cattle trucks taking the Jews. We would be walking one way across the bridge and coming the other way there were these train-loads of cattle trucks, full of Jews on their way east. We did not know at that time they were going to the gas chambers. We thought they were going off to a working party.

Thorn was a typical Polish provincial town with a big cathedral and trams and everything and a big shopping centre. It was in the news in Britain in 1980 – Thorn, now Torun – when a Polish priest was murdered by the Stasi. The Poles held their trial in Thorn and there have been quite a few pictures from it.

At the other end of the town, a road bridge had been built across the Vistula. It had been bombed by the Germans during the war, but it had been repaired and later on we would use that as well.

The first time we walked into town it was quite a shock. For something like twelve months we had never seen a woman. It was quite an 'interesting shock'. 'Helpful' shock, you might call it!

Fort 14, the hospital Fort, had a catchment area of the whole of Stalag XX-A. This area stretched 100 miles as far as Marienburg to the north and about 100 miles all the way round.

We would take in men from the big working parties and also from the big Forts. Each of the Forts had its own doctor, who handled all the usual small stuff, but we took the more serious cases that the Fort doctors could not handle.

As I have said, Fort 14 was different from the other forts in that the moat was really a moat filled with water. It had a bridge over the moat to get in and out of the Fort with a guard at the other side of the bridge. The banks had been planted with trees and quite honestly it was a very pleasant venue to have as a POW camp. The Germans kept to the other side of what looked like a small river, so we kept quite free of Germans except for once a day when they came in to hold 'Appel'.

Trouble in the theatre

I was going to say we never had any problems in the operating theatre. That is not strictly true. We did have problems in that the anaesthetics were a bit crude. Let me explain.

What we used to do first to get the patients deeply asleep was to give them an injection of Evipan, the German equivalent of the British Pentothal. This was an injection into a vein in the arm. Within eight seconds the patient would be out cold, but not deep enough to do an operation on the peritoneum – which is the stomach wall. They had to be deeply relaxed before it was possible to make a cut for an appendix or hernia.

Sometimes patients would stop breathing. That did mean panic stations and everybody rushed about. Let me just give an example.

I was assisting Mr Cullen operating on a chap for varicose veins. It was nothing important. Suddenly, the chap just stopped breathing and my heart sank.

Mr Cullen, very experienced in these kind of things, just said to me, 'Don't bother with that end,' the end that the other team were working on. 'The sooner we've finished our end the easier it will be for them at their end.'

So we just carried on with the operation.

Ron, Bill, David and Mr McMillan were hammering on the chap's chest and injecting chloramine and atropine and everything else they could lay their hands on until suddenly 'Uhhhh'. He started breathing again and by golly was I relieved.

Another time it happened was with a patient who had a tuberculous testis. It was quite a tricky operation. He had also got tuberculosis of the lungs, so when he stopped breathing it really was a big crisis. We really had to work hard to pull him round. But pull him round we did.

Escape from the 'Real World'

POW life was pretty grim and men would 'escape' into an unreal world. One man could not speak. He had lost his voice because, as he wrote on a piece of paper, 'There is something wrong with my throat.'

We examined him and could not find anything physically wrong at all. It was a case of hysteria. The fact was that he could not speak. What we did was to give him a full-blown operation. We went to all the fandango of pre-medical injections. Shaving his leg and his scrotum. We actually gave him a complete anaesthetic, Evipan, to put him soundly to sleep. While he was asleep we opened his mouth and scraped, pretty gruesomely, the back of his throat. It would be very sore when he came round.

When he recovered I said to him, 'We found there was a polyp and we have removed it. You should be fine now.'

'Oh, thanks,' he said – and you see he spoke.

Another one came in with a limp. By limping and favouring one leg against the other it had distorted the muscles. We had him X-rayed, and everything and there was nothing wrong with him.

We kept on telling him, 'There is nothing wrong' and he did not believe us.

We got the hang of this one as well. A new doctor arrived on the medical side. We briefed him thoroughly. He came over to the surgery and examined this chap. He turned to us and said, 'Of course there's something wrong with him. Look you've missed this,' and said some peculiar long word that he had about muscle here and muscle there or something here.

The chap turned to us and said, 'There I told you I was sick all the time and you didn't believe me.'

'Well we now do believe you, old son, but it does mean an operation through. Do you mind?'

'No, of course, I don't mind. I want to get it done.'

We got him into the surgery, gave him an anaesthetic and a 12in scar on his leg. Sewed it up and when he came round he was as right as rain. He walked perfectly normally from then on.

There is no question at all, the things that we did under those circumstances made us realise how much of the sickness is in the mind; you can help the mind to overcome the sickness.

We had another case which we thought was exactly like that. This chap had a swollen knee and we thought that was also in the mind.

What was fantastic about this chap was that he always kept on asking us if he could have some fresh fruit. Well there was no way that we could give him fresh fruit. We just did not have fresh fruit. We had lots of Red Cross fruit but it was all in tins. There was nothing we could do about that problem. The chap moaned on about it. In the end another doctor came in who was from New Zealand. He said that the man had a tuberculous knee.

At that time there was a lot of tuberculosis in New Zealand this this doctor identified it as a tuberculous knee, so we sent him off to a German TB sanatorium.

They sent him back three weeks later and said he had not got tuberculosis at all; he had a Vitamin C deficiency. In other words, he was needing fresh fruit, which the poor lad had been asking for all the time. We put him on a course of Vitamin C tablets and soon solved the problem of his swollen knee.

'Positively Positive'

Under the terms of the Geneva Convention, 'other ranks', i.e. not officers or NCOs, were expected to work. The men in Stalag XX-A worked mainly on the farms though some men worked in factories or on construction sites.

The men working on the farms usually had a large house in the village as their base with a few German guards. Each day after breakfast, they would go off to 'their' farms for the day, returning to base in the evening. They were the only fit males within sight. All the Poles, *Volksdeutsche* (local 'Germans'), were all called up.

Some of our men had to 'service' two or three young women; it was hard work, and I remember one chap coming into Fort 14 for a 'rest period'. He begged us not to send him back, but as so many men had walked back to Stalag to ask to be re-assigned to another camp, the Germans insisted that they had to be returned.

We were told that 25 per cent of the local women had gonorrhoea. It was therefore not surprising that our chaps were sent to Fort 14 for a course of antibiotics to clear this venereal disease. By that time, we had M&B 693 (Sulfapyridine) sent out by the Red Cross and it soon cured the condition.

From the British doctors' point of view, these men had caught a sexually transmitted disease and needed treatment. From the German doctors' point of view, no POW could have been allowed to have sex with the local 'German' women.

To test if these men had caught a venereal disease or not slides were made by Hugh March in our 'laboratory', from the semen collected from the penis after the prostate gland had been massaged – and that was my job! If the man had caught VD, the slide revealed 'a gram-negative staphylococcus' infection.

By very strange coincidence, accepted by both German and British doctors, ALL of these men had a gram positive, not negative, staphylococcus infection entered onto their charts, and were, therefore, not deemed to have caught a sexually transmitted disease. A face-saving exercise on the part of the German army.

No escape

I know that because of the films like *The Great Escape* everyone imagines that POWs have to escape. That is not necessarily so, as I explained in the Preface.

Officers HAVE to escape, no question, it costs a lot of money to train them and their task is to escape as soon as they can from POW camps. The same with air crew. We were neither of those. We were just other ranks, privates and gunners, and we were told by the senior British officer that we were NOT to escape.

As I mentioned in the Preface, the reason was very simple: any British soldier trying to escape was helped by the Poles. Any Polish civilian found helping a POW to escape was shot. And there was absolutely no justification for anybody getting killed just to let an untrained private or gunner get away. Therefore, we were under strict instructions not to escape.

There were two occasions when that situation did not really apply. One of them was what we called the Straff (Punishment) Camp escapees.

Nearby there was a punishment camp where the punishment was so severe that men would subject themselves to self-inflicted injuries. For example, one group who worked on a railway siding pushing trucks up and down the siding would put a foot on the railway line and let the truck run over it. This would mangle their foot, but it meant that they were sent into hospital.

Another trick was to use a syringe and inject petrol into an arm, which made the arm balloon up with septicaemia. What a state they were in.

They also found a root which when rubbed into the eye caused the eye to come up like a balloon. The risks they took!

These lads were sent to my surgical ward. The last thing they wanted to do was to go back to the Straff Camp. But did not want to get home to Britain because they knew they were not allowed to go home to Britain from Poland. What they did want to do was to get into one of the big Forts. The big Forts had 2,000–3,000 men and could always do with a few spare odd bods.

Let me explain what happened with two men in my ward.

First of all, we had teams which went to Stalag to collect Red Cross parcels. We had a track cart and Harry used to lead a team of people to push the cart to Stalag, load it up with Red Cross parcels and bring it back. That had to be done every week.

As the team walked up the road they would meet chaps from other Forts also pushing their carts to pick up Red Cross parcels. One of the lads from my ward, who did not want to go back to the Straff camp, joined Harry's team. On the way, they came across the other team on the way back to their Fort, laden with Red Cross parcels

They all got in a big gaggle in the middle of the road. When they left, one of THEIR chaps was pushing OUR truck and came back to Fort 14. My chap was pushing THEIR truck and went back to Fort 15 and was lost within the 2,000–3,000 men who were there. So he did not go back to the Straff camp. The Germans were very cross.

The other one was even more amusing than that.

Two things happened simultaneously: an ambulance arrived to take patients, who were cured, back to Fort 13, and two German guards arrived to take one of my men back to the Straff camp.

PHASE EIGHT

He begged me to do something about it. He was a big husky fellow.

One of the chaps who was due to go back to Fort 13 was a small lad so I said to the big fellow, 'OK, tip out your kit bag' and said to the small lad, 'Get into the kit bag. What's your name?'

'Jones.'

To this the big husky bloke, who was due to go back to the Straff camp, I said, 'You call yourself Jones, and carry this kit bag on your shoulder.'

And he really did. He just walked past the guards, clambered onto the ambulance with his 'kit' bag and got away with it. Now the Germans were really quite cross about this and they thought I had something to do with it. That, in fact, is another story. I was given one hour's notice to move out of Fort 14. I will tell you about that later in Phase Nine of this book.

But now the story of a real escape.

The 'great' escape

The escape concerned Mr Cullen, my doctor, and John Grieg, the RSM and camp commandant. Mr Cullen was drinking too much and John Grieg was extraordinarily ambitious and wanted to become a lieutenant.

They both decided that they had to escape and get back to Britain. If you were an officer in a men's camp you had to ask permission to escape. It took six months to get permission from the senior British officer (SBO).

Because we were in Poland, the SBO had links with the Polish underground. One winter night they walked out over the frozen moat. They caught a car that was waiting outside the Fort which took them to Danzig. There they caught a boat which took them across the Baltic to Sweden. From Sweden they flew home in the bomb bay of a Mosquito. They were home in four days. So that if you were ALLOWED to escape, bingo, you got your ticket home. We were left to handle the aftermath of their escape.

One of John Grieg's tasks as camp commandant was to go round each morning with the German guard, to check we had the full complement of people in the Fort.

The morning after the escape, the guard went in to John's room, where Graham Reed, a sergeant who shared the accommodation with John, was waiting.

The German guard stood for a time, looked at his watch and said to Graham, 'Where is the commandant?'

Graham said, 'He is not here.'

'I shall have to report this to the camp commandant, a Feldwebel,' said the guard.

'Do what you like,' said Graham.

A few minutes later, along comes the Feldwebel who was in charge of the guard house. He said, 'I understand that he is not here.'

'You are quite right,' said Graham.

'Well,' said the Feldwebel, 'we are all men. If the commandant has just gone over the wall to have a woman and will be back in two or three days I understand these things. We are all human. As long as I know what has happened I can cover it up. Will you tell me if that is what he has done?'

Graham said, 'I'm sorry, he is not here.'

So the Feldwebel said, 'I shall have to report this to Stalag.'

Graham said, 'You must do what you will.'

'There will be a terrible row,' said the Feldwebel.

'I am sorry,' said Graham, 'but he is not here.'

There was SUCH a shindig. An officer came from Stalag and screamed his way round the Fort. The moat had frozen over for winter and we had used it for ice skating. But it was now the end of the winter and it did not really matter that they broke the ice. The searched everywhere. I do not know what they did not do to try to find him. But they did not find John Grieg.

There was such a terrible row and all the guards were sent out to the Russian front. They doubled the guard, broke the ice and did everything they could.

Four days later, by which time John Grieg and Mr Cullen were back in England, the German doctor came to have an inspection of the Fort. He came once a week to argue with us about which patients were in hospital and why we had not discharged them etc. Our task was to keep the hospital full. Their task was to keep the hospital empty with the men back on the working parties.

A meeting was usually held in the office with the British and French doctors; that morning there were the doctors in the office and me.

The German doctor looked at me and said, 'Where is Mr Cullen?'

I said those wonderful words, 'He's not here.'

Well you have never heard anything like it in all your life. They either had to admit that after doubling the guard, breaking the ice, etc., an officer had escaped, or that four days previously, when they had searched the Fort inside and out, they had not realised they had lost a doctor. What a bloody row that was.

A few weeks later, we heard that they had arrived home safely. I met Tommy Cullen and John Grieg after the war.

An escape that did not come off

In Stalag, working in the offices, there were two chaps. One we called the 'Professor', as you probably imagine, that meant he was a very, very clever man, and spoke almost word-perfect German, and a thug friend of his who was into the rackets. What they did was this:

Nearby was a working party at Schneidermuele, working for Siemens, the big electrical company. With a lot of bribery – it must have been a tremendous bribe, but because these two chaps worked in Stalag where all the Red Cross parcels were, they had obviously stolen a lot of parcels to 'hand out' – they managed to get papers that showed them as being directors of Siemens. They also had a travel warrant on the railways to Switzerland.

In order to look like directors of a big company like Siemens, they went into Thorn and had brand-new suits made for them. You can imagine the rackets that these people were into to get that done.

Sure enough, one morning they dressed in their new civilian clothes with suitcases, went to Thorn Station to catch a train to Berlin on their way to Switzerland. In Berlin they were stopped by a policeman who asked for their passes. He checked them, saluted and apologised and said, 'I am very sorry, you do appreciate we meet lots of people who are not what they appear to be. Thank you very much.'

They stayed in a hotel in Berlin and did the thing in style as though they were directors of Siemens, then travelled by train to Lindau in Switzerland. I had been in Lindau on my holiday just before the war. Lindau is an island in the middle of the Bodensee, Lake Constance. You get to it by railway over a viaduct. From Lindau, boats sail across the lake to Switzerland. The professor and this thug mate of his handed in their tickets at Lindau Station. They could actually see the boat they were wanting to catch.

An old boy, a station ticket collector, said, 'Excuse me, Sir, I am very sorry, I do apologise but I would be deeply grateful if you would just come into the office.' He looked at their passes and said, 'Your passes are absolutely correct and I am probably going to be in terrible, terrible trouble, but if you don't mind please I would like the station master to come and talk to you.' That was the end of it. They got caught and were sent back to Thorn to spend some time in the 'bunker'.

They asked the ticket collector, 'Please tell us how did you do it, how did you know?'

'Well sir' he said, 'It was very simple, you were dressed in brand-new civilian clothes, but they were what I would call a Polish provincial cut. If you were directors of Siemens, as you purported to be, you would have been wearing London Savile Row suits.'

The sad end to that story is that the Professor, who was on the final march home with me, caught dysentery and I had to leave him behind.

Red Cross parcels

These parcels were unquestionably the item from home which saved our lives. As I have mentioned before, the first year of POW life was absolutely, indescribably, terrible. We lost a lot of men. It was so debilitating, what with the lice, starvation and the intense cold.

In June 1941, just about a year after we had been taken prisoner, Red Cross parcels started coming through and from then on came through regularly.

Previously, we had bulk parcels in tea chests which came from the Argentine, with corned beef and marmalade, which I could never eat.

Once Red Cross parcels started coming through they came through regularly which meant, without many breaks, we had them every week.

The Germans were very correct. The Nazis did not want to be seen to be short of anything. 'Of course, the prisoners must have their parcels,' they said. 'We don't need it, we're alright.'

In fact, in those early days of the war they really were alright. They had pillaged Europe, and German civilians lived extremely well. Later on it was a different story.

Our Red Cross parcels came from two sources. Britain and Canada. The Canadian parcels were transported in plywood tea chests which, after the parcels were taken out, could be converted into furniture, such as armchairs, or we used the plywood to make scenery for our shows.

The two parcels consisted of:

CANADIAN PARCEL	BRITISH PARCEL
Butter – 1lb	Margarine – ½lb
Jam	Jam
Salmon	Stew
Spam	Meat Loaf
Cheese	Cheese
Tea	Tea
Sugar	Sugar
KLIM (milk powder)	Nestles milk
Chocolate	Chocolate
Cigarettes	Cigarettes
Biscuits	Biscuits
Prunes/Raisins	Prunes/Raisins
Egg powder	Creamed rice
Soap	Egg powder
	Soap

They just transformed our lives. They supplied the extra calories that we needed.

If you looked at the list of goodies with meat, fish and a stew, which was not very filling, we had three main meals a week. As there are seven days in a week and if you tried to look after yourself on your own, you only ate well on three days a week. There was no way that you could cut a portion in half and save it and food left around was stolen, no question; you had to sleep on it or you lost it.

The result was that it was impossible for one man alone to really, satisfactorily, get on. Even two together was not enough either, because that gave only six extra meals and you still had seven days a week. The ideal number to mess together was three and in the early days Ron Dryden, Dave Thomas and I messed together. The three of us pooled our food, which demanded a great deal of self-control on our part. You did not have to look to see whether he had taken a bigger knifeful of margarine than you had or a bit more jam that you had.

In the end, of course, it did not matter, we all had so much. But in those early days it was very difficult. Nevertheless, we persevered and it did mean that each evening we could make an extra meal. That is what we did with our Red Cross parcels.

We had German coffee in the morning and we could use Red Cross biscuits and cheese for breakfast. We had the German soup for lunch and when the bread ration came along we had jam for tea. They we would make an extra meal with Red Cross food for supper.

While it was fine if three of you could pool resources, there were always some chaps who just could not do that. We had one lad in our room, there were eleven of us in the room in those days, who when the Red Cross parcels arrived, would clamber with his parcel onto the top of his bunk, turn his back on the rest of us and eat the lot that night. Well he could not lose anything that way. True, it made him sick, but he ate everything – stew, chocolate, the lot.

Then he would flog his soap for cigarettes from somebody else. That was the end of his parcel. Three days later, he'd be standing over us while we were eating supper, moaning like the clappers and pointing at us saying, 'You must have extra food, you could not save your food like that.'

He could not understand how anybody could have a little bit of discipline.

The great thing with the Red Cross parcels were the soap and cigarettes. The Germans would give their life for a bar of soap. It was extraordinary.

Their soap was made of a slimy sand. It was absolutely ghastly stuff and stank like anything. This meant that with soap, you could buy things. For example, Harry Morice arranged for the Polish women outside the Fort to do our laundry and darn our socks in return for bars of soap. We gave Harry a bar of soap a month.

The great barter business

Cigarettes were currency.

Every single item in that Fort had a value in cigarettes. A list was pinned up that said

A bar of chocolate	40 cigarettes
A pair of socks	60 cigarettes
A pair of shorts	100 cigarettes
A radio set	1,000 cigarettes

Every single thing you could think of, boots, shoes, shorts, whatever you wanted that was civilian stuff you could buy. It would come from somebody's parcel from home. You could buy literally anything.

The ultimate purchase was a lorry. We got fed up with going down to the railway station to pick up our Red Cross parcels with a hand truck and so we bought a lorry; it burnt charcoal so we had no problem with fuel.

Everything, but everything, was buyable with cigarettes. Schnapps, barrels of beer, whatever we wanted: geese, eggs, rabbits. Anything that the local people had we could buy through the German guards, who made a cut.

What used to happen was that each evening the German guard would walk around the hospital knocking on doors and asking what we wanted. We would place our order and it would be delivered the next evening. I will never forget one night in particular.

We were having supper when a guard knocked on the door, came in and said, 'Would you like a rabbit?'

We looked at each other and said, 'Yes, that's not a bad idea. Yes, let's have a rabbit.'

He put his hand in his jacket and pulled it out. It was alive, it was all wriggling. He had got it by the ears and we said, 'For God's sake kill it.'

So he just clobbered it round the back of the neck. We had rabbit stew the next day. It was lovely.

The radio set

Having a radio was *streng verboten* – strictly forbidden. If the Germans found a radio you were sent to the bunker. They did not like us to have the news.

In 1942, Willy Grant and I were in charge of the tuberculosis barrack. By that time, we had got things really organised and we had a very powerful radio set. It was kept in a suitcase in our barrack.

Every evening we would listen to the BBC World Service. We had a team. A Signals sergeant major operating the set, a journalist from the *Glasgow Record* who wrote out the evening bulletin, and Estival, our interpreter, who listened to the German news during the day.

The news bulletin that was read out in the wards each evening was an amalgam of British and German news. So we were probably better served with news than most people.

You can imagine the thrill it was for POWs to hear the news from home.

You may, or may not, know that the World Service always started with the opening bars of Beethoven's Fifth, 'Bom, bom, bom, booom, bom, bom, bom, booom. This is the World Services of the BBC bringing the news at 9 o'clock, read by – (whoever was the reader that night).' Wow, what a thing to hear.

The reason that he gave his name, very soon we could recognise the voices, was to stop the Germans from using the wavelengths for twisted propaganda.

The reason for using Beethoven's Fifth as a tuning signal was that if someone broke into a room, anywhere in Europe, the listeners could quickly switch off and claim that they were, in fact, listening to Beethoven. The signal was, in fact, Morse code for the letter 'V' for Victory, Mr Churchill's two finger sign.

'Vs' appeared all over Europe. Painted on walls and roads. Dr Goebbels, the German propaganda minister, turned the 'V' to good effect from a German point of view. He made sure that the new 'secret weapons' were called 'V weapons': V1 was the buzz bomb; V2 was the rocket; and V3 was the massive gun aimed at London.

In German, the letter 'V' stood for *Vergeltungswaffe* (reprisal weapon). It was meant to be a reprisal for the massive Allied bombing effort.

What was interesting was that we actually saw the V2 rocket being tested. On a clear summer day, we could see the contrails as they took off. Strangely enough, the first contrails we saw were crooked and we wondered what on earth caused crooked contrails. It was not until, one day, I saw a rocket lift off that I realised the reason for the crooked contrails. As the rocket lifted off, the contrails went straight up to the sky. Within a few minutes the different air streams at different heights broke it up to look crooked. At night we could watch the red glow of the rocket engine as it passed over our hut miles above.

Willy and I also had our own little radio sets, little crystal sets, with ear phones. We had an earphone each to listen to the dance music beamed from the local Thorn Radio Station. So we did not do badly.

PHASE EIGHT

The German commandant in the guard house knew we had radios. If he heard on the grapevine that we were going to be searched by the German military police, he would rush madly round the Fort saying, '*Der Abwehr Kommt. Der Abwehr Kommt.*' And we would say 'Thank you very much' and hide the radio away. The last thing the German commandant wanted was to get into trouble because we had radios, so it was better for him to warn us.

Usually the Germans would not come anywhere near the tuberculosis block. Not always though. Later in 1944 we had a slightly different set up and, on that occasion, I nearly got caught.

The German commandant warned us that the Abwehr were on his heels. I grabbed the set, in the suitcase, and walked up the outside of the hut and stepped into one of the rooms.

I lifted up a patient who was dying of lung cancer, pushed the suitcase under his back to prop him up like a pillow. At that very second, a German followed me into the room. I turned and said '*Hier ist schwer TB*' – very sick TBs, he fled. There was no way he was going to search that place – not at all.

The poor lad died three or four days later but he certainly saved us from a lot of hassle that night.

What was interesting, with the German radio, was that if you listened to it for any length of time they would stop, every now and then, and give a special announcement. The translation was: 'Over the state area there are no enemy airplanes.' They did that to keep people working, because everybody had to work flat out.

They would also tell if a raid was taking place.

'Enemy planes over Bremen' or 'over Brunswick' or 'wherever'.

That was quite extraordinary. The Germans wanted everybody to work hard and told them where the raid was going to be. So that only when the raid was overhead should people stop work.

I remember I was in bed sick with measles (see later note), and I heard a big American Air Force raid in progress. There was a first division raid against Hamburg. Then the main raid went in and hammered Berlin.

The first night that I ever heard the British radio in the POW camp was to hear of the British landing in Sicily. I went back to my bed and cried. I thought, 'there I was listening to the 9 o'clock news in a POW camp in Poland and so was my dad at home 3,000 miles away.'

It really was quite a thing.

Measles

I have just mentioned my listening to the news whilst I was recovering from measles. You might wonder how in an adult prison camp, I caught measles.

It was all Sergeant Harry Morice's fault!

Harry as I have said previously was the 'Man of Confidence' and because at the time, the Germans had not allocated him a separate position in the camp hierarchy, he had to live in my surgical barrack, ostensibly as my assistant.

Also, as I have said, one of his responsibilities was to collect our Red Cross parcels from Stalag. Being a very friendly chap, he used to give the Polish children he met on his way to Stalag, some chocolate from our parcels, much to their great delight. He did not catch measles himself but he carried it back to me! Remember, I was a medical orderly in a surgical ward.

My doctor, Mr Cullen, was a surgeon. I reported to him that I had sweated so much that I had to 'dry out' my bedding each night in the 'delouser' – the heat chamber. It took three days complaining on my part before he allowed me to meet another medical doctor who immediately diagnosed measles.

Harry was so embarrassed that he had me moved over to a private room in the 'infectious' barrack and made sure I was comfortable. In his store he had loads of special invalid food. He fed me on tinned oysters, peaches, etc. etc. I lived like a fighting cock. I was almost sorry to get back to my ward. It was the first 'rest period' I had had for years.

Wine

My father used to make wine, because his father, my grandad, who had a farm in Buckinghamshire, used to make wine. So I knew how to make wine.

In Fort 14, one of the things we had supplies of from Red Cross parcels was raisins and raisins, after all, are little grapes.

We also had yeast tablets, which we could easily get hold of working, as we did, in the surgery, and sugar. Well, honey really, also from the Red Cross parcels. We received tins of honey instead of jam occasionally.

Honey, sultanas, raisins and yeast tablets in a wooden bucket make a very palatable white wine!

There were two of us who knew how to make wine in Fort 14. Jackie Cooper was the other one, a country lad from Buckinghamshire. The two of us palled-up and made bottles of wine which were very drinkable. It was a bit of fun anyway.

As soon as we started this, everyone thought, 'Wowee, what an idea.'

The only trouble was that there were not many wooden buckets in the Fort, and Jackie Cooper and I had bagged the only two that were available. Everyone else started using galvanised buckets!

Alcohol removes the galvanising.

The result was that the taste was revolting; however, alcohol is alcohol. In those days we had not things as well organised as later on and so everybody drank it.

Then they found big earthenware jars and started making wine in them. The idea of making wine soon spread to the other Forts. Before very long, some men started drinking it while it was still fermenting. In fact, in one great booze-up when they got to the bottom of the jar they ate the yeast as well. No wonder they were sick.

This may sound hard to believe, but shoe blacking has a certain amount of alcohol mixed with it and if you put the tin of shoe blacking on a stove and melted it, it goes to a liquid which the men drank. Yuk!

I suppose that is no different from that first year when we did not have cigarettes. They found a bit of newspaper, dried leaves, crushed them up and rolled them in the newspaper and smoked it. God knows what it did to their lungs.

By train across Germany

From time to time we would gather patients together who needed special treatment. Two different kinds of patients – one tuberculosis and the other mental cases. They were sent to sanatoriums in Germany. Two German guards would be appointed to go with the party of probably twenty patients, plus one British medical orderly and one interpreter.

I managed to do two such trips – I was very fortunate in that respect.

My first turn came in November 1942. A group of tuberculosis cases were to be taken to a sanatorium in the Bohemian mountains. The railway station authorities would lay on a coach, a whole coach, in a siding in the station at Thorn. We would go down with the ambulance first of all to take paillasses and blankets and food. Later, the patients would come down and we would make them comfortable.

The German trains had wooden seats and we put the patient on a paillasse and covered him with blankets. They were quite comfortable. Two chaps for each compartment.

In one compartment at the end of the carriage would be me, the medical orderly, the interpreter and the two guards with all the food and everything. When our train came into the station the authorities would hitch us up and off we went. Posen was usually the first stop.

There they would unhook us. We would get hot water from the German Red Cross in the station. I took Dixies with me, big Dixies, and I made a hot drink.

Sometimes, if the train was shunted off the main line for an hour or so, we would go to the engine and persuade the driver to let some steam come from his tap and fill the Dixie up with hot water that way. We made the patients very comfortable. We had plenty of good food with plenty of Red Cross parcels. Slowly, but surely, we would drift across Germany.

A note of interest, all the German trains had *Räder müssen rollen für den Sieg* (wheels must turn for victory) painted on their sides.

The other place we always went through was Cottbus, which was a major rail junction. This time we went south to Chemnitz and Zwichau. When the train finally stopped at a little wayside station, the sanatorium sent ambulances to collect the patients. We went back with them.

This particular hospital was run by French doctors. They were very pleasant and put us up for the night. We had a room each and were made very comfortable. Let's face it, we were free. We could have escaped. But we were medical orderlies doing a job we had had our orders and therefore we did not. So that was that.

Next morning, because I was a medical orderly and was in charge, one of the guards said to me, through Estival the interpreter, 'I have two passes, one which says we do not have to be back in Thorn for three days and the other is a pass which lets us go anywhere on the German railway system.

PHASE EIGHT

I live in Dusseldorf and I would love to take you to meet my family, but I am afraid the British are bombing it and I would not like you to be bombed by your own people and also if we got caught out and did not get back in time there would be a great row. Nevertheless, we have got this ticket. Now if you want to, of course, you can go back to Thorn immediately. We can be in Thorn tomorrow morning. Where would you like to go?'

Well, let's face it. If you were in Germany where would you go? Berlin, of course. So I said, 'Can we go to Berlin?'

'Yes, sure,' he said, 'I have a friend in the Kommandaturer. He will put us up for the night.'

So off we went – via Leipzig.

On the way from the sanatorium to Leipzig we got on a local train that wandered across the country. They had a woman guard on this train who clambered into our compartment to boast about how they were winning the war. 'Look at all the autobahns,' and 'aren't we clever, we Germans?' She was doing a real bit of propaganda.

So, being the rotten swine that I am, I did not say anything at all but merely turned round and lifted down a Red Cross parcel from the roof rack. I opened it and started showing her the stuff.

In the end we had her in tears, she was sobbing her heart out.

'All you POWs with all this food, this meat and milk and chocolate, and my children at home haven't anything of that sort. It's all wrong.' She really was in a hell of a state and I thought, 'so much for you mate, so much for you.'

Leipzig is the largest railway station in Europe. Trains come in from the north, south, east and west. We went into the Red Cross hall. It was the most extraordinary sight. It was a huge hangar of a place, full of German soldiers all waiting to catch their train to go back to the Russian front. These lads knew that they were going to go back to what, eventually for most of them, was either death or a prisoner of war. It was a frightful atmosphere.

We sat at a table, two guards, Estival and me. Estival called over a German Red Cross girl in her white uniform with a red cross. I gave her one of our Dixies and asked her to make some cocoa for us.

'Here's the cocoa and here's the milk.'

Well, she was stunned. She may never, in her life, have seen cocoa, because the Germans had this system for years before the war of 'guns before butter', as I had seen on holiday in 1939, which meant that everybody had to make enormous sacrifices in food, so that they could have guns and it was possible the girl had never seen cocoa.

I said, 'Make it very strong, put in 5 big spoonfuls,' and told her how to make it.

She went off with it, came back and said, 'I've made it ever so well and I used nearly half the packet.'

'Oh,' I said, 'That's fine. I am glad you have made it well. You keep the rest.' It was all good propaganda.

The girl was almost in tears, seriously, there were tears in her eyes. Off she went.

Then one of the German guards made what I think was a grave error. He had been drinking his cup of cocoa, obviously we looked after the guards – who wouldn't? I mean we were all soldiers together. He said to me, 'Over there is a Feldwebel who has been good to me. He is just off to the eastern front. Would you mind if I gave him a cup of cocoa?'

'No, you do that,' I said.

So the guard filled his cup and started to walk across this hall to this Feldwebel. Well, the delicious smell of cocoa wafted across the hall. You could have heard a pin drop. All eyes were on this chap.

He realised his mistake as soon as he started walking. It was the most frightful business.

Let's face it; here we were POWs with food that they could not get and we were giving it away, largesse like, and they were going back to the eastern front to fight the Russians.

My golly.

I said, 'Quick, let's get out of here' and we grabbed our Dixie and fled.

We caught the train to Berlin and that too was interesting. It was filled with civilians. In our carriage there was a German submariner, he was off to get his boat at Kiel or somewhere, with his girlfriend. I looked at him and having listened to the British news I knew that he would not be coming back. Three-quarters of all the sailors who joined the German submarine service died.

When we arrived at Berlin it was Charlottenburg station. We got out of the main line station and climbed up onto a section of the U-bahn, which like sections of the Metro in Paris, ran above ground. We caught the train into the centre of Berlin.

PHASE EIGHT

They took us for a walk to see the sights. They kept saying, 'Look, no bombing,' because in November 1942 the RAF were never sure of bombing Germany, let alone Berlin. In the early days of the war, we were dropping bombs on France thinking that it was Germany.

Finally, we went underground on the U-bahn. We changed trains at Tiergarten and somewhere else. It was quite interesting being with all these German civilians in the underground train. Nobody said a word to us.

We were smartly dressed in brand-new British army uniforms, supplied through the Red Cross; I had all my brasses, Royal Artillery brasses, polished. Buttons polished. Gaiters blancoed. Belt blancoed. We were smart, well-dressed soldiers. No way did we look like scruffy POWs.

We finally landed up at the *Kommondantur* where we were going to stay for the night.

The *Kommondantur* was a huge, huge barracks called the *Bendlerblock*, where men were being trained, marching up and down.

Our guard contacted his mate and asked if he could put us up for the night.

The chap said, 'Yes sure.' He gave Esti and me a nice room. It was terribly amusing.

Our guard said, 'I want good bedding.'

'Oh yes' said his mate and changed the bedding so that we had fresh paillasses and plenty of blankets.

Then our guard said, 'Don't lock the door.'

The chap said, 'Of course I am not going to lock the door. If I lock the door how can they use the washroom and everything?'

We had the run of the place. We went outside and watched the soldiers parading and marching up and down. We used the washrooms and everything and nobody said a word. Not once did we get questioned. It was quite extraordinary really.

We had a window looking out on the street and we could see all the people walking up and down. It was quite extraordinary, quite extraordinary – this was Berlin 1942.

Next day we caught the train from Berlin back to Thorn.

My next trip did not come until 9 January 1945. This time it was another lad who was my interpreter and two guards. This time we were going south again through Dresden, taking twenty patients to a mental home.

Again, the same system applied. Linking us up and wandering across the country through Posen and Cottbus again; it took us four or five days and was very pleasant really. We had plenty of food.

Nobody hassling us. The German guards were very pleasant. No problem at all. Slowly, like gypsies, we would wander across the country.

Finally, when we had taken our patients to the mental home, the German guards were fairly anxious to get back this time. So off we went to catch the train. We were going to Thorn via Frankfurt-an-der-Oder. Near to Dresden we had to change trains. It was a big station. On the platform there was a restaurant, so we went in and ordered beers and because it was near Czechoslovakia they served us with real Pilsner lager. I have never tasted anything like it. It was super! It was like cream. It was nectar.

So I ordered another round of drinks. The waiter came over and said, 'There is a war on and beer like this is on short supply, but as you are soldiers – well fair enough, I don't mind getting them for you.' As he talked he cleaned the table prior to bringing the drinks.

He turned to the guards and said, 'Who are these soldiers? Hungarians?'

The reason he asked this was that we were in khaki uniforms and the only other people who wore khaki, in the German army, was either the German desert corps – and we obviously were not German desert corps – or the Hungarians.

'No,' said the guards, 'Englanders.'

So this chap said, 'Englander? Kriegsgefangener (POWs)? But they are paying for the drinks!'

'Yes,' said the German guard, 'they have more money than we have.'

Which, of course, was true because we had had Red Cross parcels, we had no shortage of anything, not anything.

So off he went and got the beers.

After we had finished our drinks, we caught a German army 'leave' train going back to the Russian front via Thorn. It was January 1945. The war ended a few months later.

The situation in Russia was desperate, desperate. The atmosphere was like a tinder box. The train was full of men going back to their death or POW and they all knew it. The two guards were just going back to a POW camp and they would be safe. The atmosphere was horrendous. So much so that the German guard said to me, 'I am sorry. I cannot stay on this train a moment longer. Can we get off at the next station?'

PHASE EIGHT

So at the next station off we got. Then we were caught because it was the last train of that day. There were no trains the next day as it was Sunday.

So we had to stay on the station, in the waiting room, for a whole day with a load of Hitler *Jugend* before we could catch the train back to Thorn on the Monday morning.

We did not mind. We had plenty of food and we were alright. The German guards had been terrified out of their lives on the train. And rightly so.

In the corridor the soldiers were bumping, deliberately, into the guards and trying to knock them down. They were also doing it to each other. The tension on that train you cannot conceive. There was nothing on the Allied side comparable to being sent back to the Russian front.

From the train, we could see some strange things, such as, for example, at Dresden passing all the huge steel works there. Although there were bombing raids in which, theoretically, you turned out the light, there is no way you can stop a steelworks with its blast furnaces and everything. That is why they could be seen from the sky.

I remember passing a huge aerodrome with Luftwaffe fighter planes Junker 88s with Yargi aerials which was their radar – they called it Lichtenstein. The German radar was better than ours and they had been shooting our bombers down at almost unacceptable limits on our part. They had been really decimating our chaps. In order to stop that carnage, the RAF was forced to drop 'window'.

'Window' was very thin strips of aluminium, cut to the right length, to disrupt the German radar. The reason why the British had not used it before was because we were afraid that the Germans would use it against us. At that time of the war, towards the end, only our bombers were bombing. No German bombers were bombing England. The losses were all one-sided. All the trees were festooned, like Christmas trees, with this thin aluminium tape.

Another interesting point about the journey. Just before we left the camp we had been listening to the news. We heard that the Russians had completely surrounded Tarnapol (now known as Ternopil). Once it was surrounded, in those days, that was the end of it.

The Russians claimed to have taken 100,000 German soldiers prisoners or that they were killed. If you were taken prisoner by the Russians that pretty well meant dead because very few German soldiers came back from Russia. Tarnapol was in my mind.

You can imagine my consternation when in the train, with all these civilians, one of them, a woman, was talking about her man. 'My man is in Tarnapol,' she said. I thought, 'well good luck to you love, you will never see him again.'

She was also talking quite openly about the bombing.

This is the interesting part.

The Germans never really beat our people when they bombed London. True Londoners were frightened but they still went to work each day and still walked through the streets that had been bombed. And so it was with the Germans. The more we dropped bombs on them the more they seemed to resist and fight back. In fact, the productivity of the German armament industry increased throughout the whole of the war. Every month they increased their productivity even though we were bombing some of their factories.

It was most interesting listening to these German women talking about being bombed in Frankfurt-an-der-Oder. How everybody went down to the deep shelters and sang songs. It is difficult to be with people and listen to them and their suffering and not feel sorry for them.

Showtime

I was a production manager in an advertising agency before the war. I was also a member of the 28th Willesden Scouts who used to produce some very find shows based upon Ralph Reader's 'Gang Shows'. In fact, ours was the only show that Ralph could bear to watch. I used to help in scene shifting.

As an advertising man I was well versed in using words and visuals. With soap and cigarettes from Red Cross parcels we could buy anything and so men who could play the guitar or the saxophone, the clarinet or the trumpet or the drums, could buy these musical instruments.

Fort 14 was a hospital Fort and many of the men were regular army stretcher bearers. In the British army, stretcher bearers double as bandsmen. Therefore, because we had a lot of stretcher bearers working in the hospital, ipso facto, we had a lot of bandsmen. Very fine bandsmen, trained at Kneller Hall. Really professional, top class bandsmen. As well as playing military marches most of them could also play dance music, jazz and so on.

In August 1941, somebody put together a show in Fort 14. It was a shambles.

PHASE EIGHT

It took hours to shift the scenery; it was faltering and stumbling. We had a staff meeting. I stood up and said, 'It was shambolic; you ought to be ashamed of yourselves.'

So they said, 'Well can you do better?'

'Of course, I can do better. I'll put on the next show,' I said.

So I went away and wrote a show which I called *Gangway*. It was the first show I had ever put on as a POW. Though we could buy musical instruments, we had not had music sent to us as yet – so we did not have any music.

I remembered the songs that Jessie Matthews sang in her show 'Gangway' and one of these top-ranking bandsmen, Geoff Aitken, could interpret my lah-lah-lah da-da-da-da-da-da da-da-da diddle-diddle-diddle-dee-dee-dee. So with just me humming the tune, him taking down the melody by tapping out single notes on the piano he orchestrated it for the full dance orchestra. He was that clever. And so we had music.

I wrote the script and included plenty of songs. The staff were the cast. We had some quite good singers and fellows who made super 'women'! I played a part: I was the villain of the piece.

The basic story of *Gangway* was about going home, going down the gangway of the ship bringing us home. Not that a ship ever did bring me home, but anyway we used the idea of a ship bringing us home.

The story followed the hero, a POW who, when he arrived home, found that his girl had gone out with a rotten soldier and left him in the lurch – which was a dastardly thing to do!

It was a simple plot, merely a vehicle for playing good music with a little bit of dialogue.

We had costumes made up from what we could find. You wanted a grey flannel suit? Who had a grey blanket? We had plenty of tailors who could make a suit out of a blanket.

As far as the scenery was concerned, we had scenic artists, super artists, who painted whatever scenery we wanted.

Based on the Gang Shows, I had a middle curtain as well as the main curtain. It takes a bit of time to change scenery so something needs to be going on in front of a middle curtain while the scenery is being changed at the back for the next big scene.

When the show opened, the main curtain went up and did not come down until the show was ended. It went all through without a hitch – without a second's delay.

As one scene opened, I was singing, 'Must you dance, every dance with the same fortunate man?'

Bill Brickell was my 'girl', or rather the one I pinched whilst the other bloke was away. Bill Finch, the handsome debonair Bill Finch, had his girl stolen by rotten old Markham.

Just picture the moment: lighting, beautiful music – and then Bill Brickell dressed as a woman steps onto the stage. I nearly stopped singing. It absolutely smacked me straight between the eyes. He was well made up, looking absolutely stunning. I was shattered.

After the show ended, the audience would not leave. They cheered and cheered and cheered, stamped their feet and cheered and refused to leave. So we put it on again; we did it straight the way through again.

All the scenery had been put back into its place. All the side flaps had gone back into place. All the costumes had gone back. It was all ready for the next night's performance, but instead of that we did it all again that night to the same audience with the doctors and padre sitting in the front. It was tremendously emotional with people crying. So much so that one chap committed suicide. We dragged him out of the moat three days later.

That was *Gangway* in 1941.

I ran it again that Christmas. What we used to do at Christmas was to put on a show on Christmas Eve and then again on Boxing Day. Nothing happened on Christmas Day of course. That day was given over to booze and food.

I timed the length of the show, so I knew how long it took to within a few minutes. I needed to be as accurate as I could because the next big event was New Year's Eve.

In our POW camp, most of the prisoners were Scotsmen. The reason for that was that few people were captured at Dunkirk as most of them got away. At Dunkirk only about 6,000 were left behind but at St Valery about 24,000 Scotsmen of the 51st Highland Division were picked up.

Therefore, with so many Scotsmen, New Year's Eve was almost a bigger thing than Christmas Day.

Knowing exactly how long the show took to run, I then started it at a time which left me half an hour or so to organise a lead into the New Year. For example, one year I did *Father Time*. Another year, a chap who had some bagpipes welcomed in the New Year playing his bagpipes.

PHASE EIGHT

Another year I did a fancy-dress parade; that would have been 1941, and 1942 would have been *Father Time*; 1943 would have been the bagpipes and I will tell you about 1944 in a minute. The point was that the tableau or whatever went on up to midnight on New Year's Eve.

At 12 o'clock the drum would do the bong-bong-bong twelve times and the place went mad.

The show had finished and there was no point in going on a second after the coming of the New Year. It was absolute mayhem. But fantastic. Fantastic. It really was.

The musical shows were a great success. In the middle of the year we used to put on a three-act play, produced by Esti. I helped with the scenery.

They were really very good.

In one of them, *The Late Christopher Bean*, the heroine was the maid. She turned out to be the wife of Christopher Bean, the artist, with all his wonderful paintings. Geoff Aitken played the part. At the end of each performance, he got himself so worked up he sobbed and sobbed.

Scenery for the plays

Making the scenery for Esti's plays was quite demanding, particularly for *The Late Christopher Bean*. You see we had to have (to follow the script), a desk with a telephone, a dresser, a series of paintings (many with detailed instructions as to how they looked) and a fireplace. To make it look homely we decided to have wallpaper!!

Everything, but everything, had to be handmade. Fortunately, we had a brilliant artist in the Fort. He cut a series of stencils for the wallpaper which, colour by colour, we painted on the wall.

Our carpenters made the tables, desk and chairs. They also made a wooden fireplace with an over-mantle. In Edwardian times, the wealthy had their fireplaces with an over-mantle made of marble. People like my mum and dad had their fireplace 'marbled' by a professional artist. We had enormous fun doing our 'marbling'.

By Christmas 1942, we had started getting music sent from England with *The Mikado* amongst the music. So for Christmas I produced *Aladdin* based on *The Mikado* music. It was great fun and it was really a splendid show.

The wigs were made out of sisal which had been unwound. Clothes and shoes were made. Costumes and scenery, all beautifully done.

One of the lads had to play the part of the princess. There was a great argument around the Fort when we were deciding who was going to take this part. This lad stamped his feet and screamed, 'I want to be the princess.'

The shows were the big event in the life of the staff of the hospital. I would plan the show during the summer and we would start rehearsing in the autumn. It was a wonderful social activity; a marvellous thing for the staff of the hospital to do. It gave us a focal point; it gave us something of great interest to do during those winter months leading up to Christmas. It really was a big thing.

We would invite the staff from other Forts to come and see our shows as they invited us to go to their Forts to see their shows.

At Christmas 1943 we did *Magic Carpet*. We had lots of music. It was the music that gave me the idea to do the show, because the show was only a vehicle for the songs. New York with American songs, *Down Mexico Way* and *A Desert Island*. The words only linked the songs together really, with nice costumes and super scenery.

It was a wonderful event for the patients. Many of these patients had been on working parties and seen nothing like these shows. It was an absolutely stunning eye-opener to most of them. Many of them had almost forgotten how to speak English because they had been working out on a farm with the Germans all the war. Though they had not necessarily had a tough time, they certainly had not seen anything like our shows. The cast would do little jokes of their own.

Loft Lane had quite a difficult part to play, and at the end of it he seemed to mop his forehead and squeeze his handkerchief and about a gallon of water came out of it. He had very carefully loaded his handkerchief with water beforehand and so gave it a good squeeze. The whole place fell apart with all this water all rushing about.

In another case, one of the fellows had to sing *Salome*. Well there are two versions, the clean one – which he was supposed to sing – and the extraordinary version, which he was not supposed to sing; which, of course, is what he did.

With the padre sitting in the front row. However, I am sure the padre enjoyed it.

PHASE EIGHT

At Christmas 1944, we sincerely hoped the war was going to finish in 1945, although we did not know for sure. The show we did was called *The Ghost of Castle Urquhart*.

I wanted something really spectacular this time. So I said to Harry Morice, 'I want some really super costumes and lovely scenery. I want more paint. I want a really good job this time.'

'OK,' says Harry.

A few days later, he said to me, 'Come into town tonight.' Well charming, just 'come into town tonight'.

We went down to the guardhouse and go ourselves a guard and off we went into Thorn. It did cost us a few cigarettes!

We went to the State Theatre, into the place they keep the costumes and I was allowed to choose the costumes for the show: crinolines, a hunter's uniform ... It was absolutely fantastic.

All packed up in a great big wicker basket and sent up to the camp.

I also wanted some more paper; the backcloths were made of brown paper. I will never forget going into this shop just before Christmas. We were in the queue and there were people in front asking for brown paper and being told, 'No paper, there is a war on.'

Harry walked forward with a bar of soap in his hand, which he put on the counter, and then he said, 'Have you got any brown paper?'

'How many sheets would you like, Sir?' said the chap serving.

No argument. Harry produced so much paint, in barrels, that we had enough to share it out among the other Forts.

I must admit that this was the show I really wanted to be great.

I drafted the scenario, but got the script written by Ernie Reoch, who later became the lead writer of the *Glasgow Record*. He and Estival wrote the script between them.

It was a more sophisticated script than I could produce, I still have a copy of it. Unfortunately, I have only got two photographs of that particular show, because after the show I went off to Dresden on 9 January and on 20 January, when I went on the march, the photographs had not come through.

I got hold of two in 1950 from Harry Morice who just happened to be shown the advance copies by the German who had taken the photographs.

It was the most fantastic show that we had ever put on, with nice costumes, good scenery and a good script. We had an extraordinary orchestra. They really were professional, really professional.

I just produced it and there it was.

The great thing was the lead into New Year's Eve. I thought, I am going to do a review of the war. So, as a middle curtain scene, I used a newspaper boy selling newspapers. By his side was a life-sized calendar with all the years of the war, 1939, 1940, 1941, 1942, 1943, 1944, 1945.

As people came in to buy their paper they would stop and talk about the particular year on view.

'Do you remember Hitler's speech? When he said whatever he said.'

What was amazing really was that sitting in the front row were eight German censors, people who spoke English perfectly and censored our letters, and the German commandant. So we talked about the war with the lad selling the newspapers, tearing the page off the big calendar, revealing the next year, with the Germans listening, without comment.

This was taking place on New Year's Eve 1944/1945. Only a few days after Christmas.

One of the people buying a newspaper said, 'Wasn't that a super speech by the king this year?'

The only way we could have heard the king's speech was on the radio – except that, strictly speaking, radios were forbidden.

One of the tasks of these German censors was to stop any news getting through to us. Talk about two fingers up and flaunting it. The king's speech for Christmas was read out very movingly. It was a very emotional moment.

'What will 1945 bring?,' says the paper boy. 'Will it bring more war, or will it bring the torch of liberty?'

And bursting through this life-size calendar of 1945 comes a lad dressed up as the Statue of Liberty with a torch of sparklers.

We had had a hell of a job lighting them, but light them we did.

It brought the bloody place down. There were people sobbing their hearts out, there were the Germans cheering because they wanted to see the end of the war. It was the most emotional moment ever.

I spoke to a corporal who had been on a working party. He had had a tough time. He had had a really snide German who had really pushed him and who could hardly speak English.

He was standing there, with tears streaming down his face, saying, 'Look at all those Germans in the front row. How do they get away with it?'

And I said, 'We had them to tea beforehand so don't worry about them.'

But he said, 'How have you got away with it?'

PHASE EIGHT

And that was it. He had had such a tough war, with such a bastard of a German pushing him all the time, and here we had got away with murder.

Talk about flaunting it in front of the Germans in a prison camp.

The point is that we DID get away with it. We had always got away with it. So we continued to get away with it.

But what an evening …

After the shows, particularly on New Year's Eve night, there were great parties and a great carrying on.

Under POW conditions, because of the Red Cross parcels, we were able to get what we wanted. Whatever we wanted to drink we could buy. It did mean that we had to go very carefully though, otherwise it could have gone too far.

Although conditions in our Fort were very reasonable, while there was a war on there were far worse places to be than in Fort 14 in Thorn; but the chaps were away from home and five years is a long time. The result was that towards the end we were having parties where people got so drunk that they were ill. In fact, we had one fellow who died as a result of drinking too much.

Harry and I were no drinkers. I restrained from drinking because I felt it was unwise to lose control of oneself. Harry and I were always sober, quite jolly with it, but sober, dead sober. The result was it was very common for us to be the only medical staff available of an evening in case they had been an emergency. No other barrack had anybody who was not blind drunk. Doctors and all.

Harry and I used to mop it up in the end and carry them back to their beds on stretchers.

It was all getting a bit fraught; in fact, on one occasion they started getting drunk on Christmas Eve, they then had a party every night and were drunk every night until 15 January which was somebody's birthday, when the staff of the Fort toasted the king with champagne.

They would hold a party in one barrack and the next night in another barrack and the next night another one. They did the rounds.

After that we decided it would be better to stop it because, otherwise, it was just going too far. It was just going mad, you understand? Drunk after drunk after drunk after drunk, it should have killed more people than it did.

So we stopped it.

Study in a POW camp.

It was possible to take professional exams in a POW camp. Under the authority of the Red Cross, the SBO would arrange for exams to be taken under the strictest conditions.

It was also possible to study for other exams, but, as far as I know, there were no exams for advertising.

Before the war, what studying I had done was at the London School of Printing. In the UK, advertising had stemmed from printing newspapers.

When I got home, I found that it was possible to sit for professional qualifications and I became a member of the Institute of Practitioners in Advertising, having studied for and subsequently taken the exam in November 1949.

Nevertheless, I asked the Swiss and Swedish Red Cross people to send me books on advertising. This they did and I had a small library of American books, most of which were titled *Advertising and Marketing*. In America, marketing stemmed from advertising and I became marketing director of my advertising agency in 1958! So the books helped a lot.

Records

Whilst I was working in the surgical barrack at Fort 14, my bed was by the window, which was open all the summer. A grassy bank outside the window led down to the moat which looked like a river. It was a very pleasant place to be.

At night, I could hear the trams clanking along in Thorn. That was very nostalgic, it reminded me of home.

The other thing that we did that was nostalgic was to play records. We would put the light out. Somebody would have the wind-up record player and play dreamy records. You would hear blokes in the ward sniffling. They all had a quiet weep, but I suppose it did not do anybody any harm.

We would lie back and listen to German records in those early days. The British ones did not come through until later. We knew all the latest German songs.

Records from home finally arrived, and Jimmy Lawton, who had classical records sent to him, would have a classical evening – a Beethoven evening or a Mozart evening. That is how I first got my love for classical music. It made for a very pleasant evening.

We had, in Fort 14, marvellous musicians so that we could get an interesting talk on a piece of music, then hear the music. It was very enjoyable.

In the ward we played Glen Miller, Artie Shaw and Tommy Dorsey on Columbia wind-up portable gramophones, that is the kind sent out by the Red Cross to chaps whose parents could afford to do that. They did share it all around with everybody, so we all heard the records, all heard the latest music.

Talking of music

We used to have music festivals where the dance bands that we had would play their special pieces. We would all vote for who was the best dance band in the Stalag. They were fantastic events.

Some of these dance bands from the big Forts were like Glen Miller's band, twenty or thirty strong, with the players moving in unison. Most of them were professional musicians. They were decked out in uniforms with decorated music stands. The music was of a very high quality. Occasionally, they would come down to Fort 14 to give 'open air' shows to the patients.

New glasses

When I joined the British army, I had to be supplied with a new pair of glasses. They had to have very thin sides suitable to fit under a gas mask. I was in Dursley at the time and was taken to Bristol to have the new glasses made. The utter oaf of an optician made me a pair of glasses which were absolutely useless; they had pebble lenses for my myopia.

I refused point blank to wear them and when I arrived in the POW camp I was still wearing my own civilian glasses. During 1943 I needed new glasses – eyes do change during the early twenties.

I was taken to the optician Werner Schmeichel in Thorn and got new glasses. They were excellent and as smart as I could have wished. I was treated no differently from any other customer. The receipt shows that I paid 5.40 marks in Lagergeld, which the optician must have changed into real marks at Stalag.

Photographs

I suspect that the first photographs the Germans took of us in July 1941 were for propaganda purposes. We did not mind. We could send them home; my father had them published in the local *Willesden Chronicle*.

We had just been issued with new uniforms. We were louse-free, we had Red Cross parcels and those of us who had survived that first, horrendous winter, were in good shape.

Harry got me a camera of my own. I took some photos of 'our' hut and garden and the moat, none of which the Germans had photographed. I handed the camera back to Harry to pass on to the escape committee when the officers were in Fort 15.

Photographs of our shows, etc., were taken for us by the German guards to whom we gave cigarettes.

It is true that if we wished to keep copies of the photographs we had to have them seen and stamped by the censor. They stamped *Stalag XX-A Gepruft* (censored) and their number on each. Even my own special photographs have a German censor stamp on them, but only because the censor came to have 'tea' with us.

The 'Goons'

This was the name we gave our German guards.

When we were first captured, we were taken POW by Totenkopf of the SS, and they did all they could to help the wounded. We were then passed over to the Pioneer troops, second-class soldiers who kicked us all the way through the first march into Germany. They were really stinking vicious. Because they were 'nobodies' they tried to show us that they were 'somebodies' and I suppose they were happy about it.

Then when we got to Thorn it was a different kettle of fish. Poland was an occupied country and therefore the German guards were actually living in an enemy country and we, the POWs, were in a friendly country. Britain had gone to war to help Poland, so it was a paradoxical situation.

Mostly, the German soldiers, the Wehrmacht, were correct. They did not have much to do with us. They were on the other side of the wire. We only saw the one or two who came in to count us each day.

PHASE EIGHT

I do remember a man who we actually called 'the bastard'. He really was a pig and would kick and shout and scream, but that was his inadequacy, was it not? They had to show off like that.

Because Thorn was a garrison town, the German troops were being trained for Barbarossa, the war against Russia, which started on 22 June 1941.

German troops, like American troops, sing songs. They used to sing everything every time they marched. They were very good marching songs – 'We march against England' was their favourite song. We could watch the German troops marching up and down, singing. It was quite interesting.

Because it was a garrison town, they had a garrison theatre and I remember being taken two or three times to watch a film, *White Horse Inn* was one I think, and watched the newsreel.

Frostbite

One problem which arose from the intense cold of a Polish winter was frostbite. Unless you had good warm gloves it was a high probability that you would get frostbitten fingers. We had quite a few Frenchmen with this complaint.

On one occasion, through a piece of Nazi nastiness, I had to deal with frozen toes. Young Eames, who had been my interpreter at Danzig, was an interpreter for a working party. Refusing to play a part in a particularly nasty piece of Nazi-mindedness, he was kept standing for hours in the snow by the German camp commandant. The result was frostbitten toes. We kept him in Fort 14 for so long, to give him a good long rest, that I ended up treating his back for sunburn!

Frostbite, in the severe cases that I saw, resulted in the ends of the fingers or toes turning black, like pieces of coal. After months of care, the pink 'live' flesh separated from the calcified 'dead' black, solid, finger and toe tips. Eventually, I used a pair of shears to cut through the bone between the 'live pink' and the 'coal black' pieces.

The turning point

We noticed the difference immediately. The defeat of Stalingrad in January 1943 was, for Germany, the turning point of the war.

Hitler had promised the German people that Stalingrad would be a victory. Instead it was a defeat: 250,000 Germans went into the horror of Stalingrad; 190,000 were captured by the Russians. After the war, only 6,000 returned to Germany.

On 23 October 1942, the British had broken through at El Alamein and in May the whole of the German Desert Corps surrendered at Tunis with another 250,000 troops of the German and Italian forces captured, of whom most returned to their homes after the war. So, bad though it was for Germany in North Africa, it did not in any way, have the impact of Stalingrad.

Before Stalingrad, all the Germans we met supported Hitler, though they could not all have been ardent Nazis. After Stalingrad, only the Nazis supported Hitler. The transformation from pro-Hitler to anti-Hitler was pronounced.

Towards the 'End of the Era'

The Germans were getting very hungry. There is no doubt about it, food was very short.

British soldiers are awful. As soon as they have food they throw it away. They waste it. The result was we had a lot of food that was being thrown away, not eaten.

The Germans set up a swill bin, where all this food could be collected. They decided that they would collect this swill, buy a pig and feed the swill to it. As soon as we got to hear about this, broken glass was very carefully sprinkled on top of the swill bin.

The other episode was really stark.

In the early days, we were fed on barley and swede and we got so that we would never again eat barley.

On this occasion, one of the German guards went to our cook and said, 'You POWs are very well fed and you never bother to eat your barley. I know for a fact that you have been saving it and not using it. You now have an unopened sack of barley in the cookhouse. In the guard house we are very hungry and we would be glad to make a soup of that barley. Could we please have it?'

The cook did not say a word, but put the sack on his shoulder, walked out and threw it in the moat and said, 'Fuck you mate!'

PHASE EIGHT

By 1943, things had become very tough for the Germans on the eastern front. Most of our guards had stripes to show that they had been wounded two or three times on the eastern front. I remember well one Under Officer who had been wounded twice at Sebastopol. He told us the most terrifying stories about what it was like in the battle on the eastern front.

The Russians won by their overwhelming mass of soldiers. This chap told of sitting behind a machine gun and firing and firing until it got red hot and seized up. They had to run for it, because no matter how many Russians you killed, more came on and kept on coming on and on and on.

No wonder the Russians lost 13 million, killed by the Germany army in the war. Stalin ordered the death of soldiers and civilians to as many again.

Another story we heard was from a chap who had been stationed in Leningrad up in the north. In the harsh winter, Lake Ladoga was frozen. From the Russians' point of view, with the lake frozen solid, they were able to free Leningrad by driving lorries across the lake to by-pass the German lines.

The Germans did everything they could to stop them. The result was that the front line went across the lake. This chap described to us how they were literally dug into the ice.

They were on duty for twenty-four hours at a time. Fog comes off the ice. He described how on edge he felt. Then through the icy fog could be seen figures coming towards you.

The whole idea of sleeping and living out on the ice really sort of shakes me.

It was tough for both sides. The east front for both sides was so horrendous. Nothing the allies had was comparable to that.

Games time

At Fort 14 we had two football teams; we had to play against each other. Harry had hired a field just outside the Fort and fitted it out with proper goal posts and netting and everything.

What would happen was that the German guard would come down and say, 'I want to choose a team tonight. I'll have Ginger and I'll have "fatty".' This was me because my weight had gone back up to 15½ stone. He'd choose his team, and that would be one team and then the others would play them. Next night someone else would come and choose a team. It did not matter to us, it was all good fun.

The Poles came from miles around to watch us play. With all these Scotsmen around, we had blokes who played football professionally.

I played full back. A great big hulking great fellow, I was a real stopper. So football was a big sport.

The other big sport in the summer was swimming.

About a mile up the road, there was a large disused quarry. It was overgrown with grass – and formed a very pleasant lake with a grassy bank. We used to go swimming there in the evening after a game of football.

We would get out our swimming costumes and towels, all bought with cigarettes, and go to the guard house and say, 'We want a guard.' They would fall over themselves to act as our guard. What we needed was someone to look after our clothes to stop them from being stolen by the Poles.

We would stroll up to the quarry and go swimming. It was absolutely fantastic.

In the winter, the moat used to freeze so we got skates from Sweden. We used to have ice hockey and ice skating. That is where I learnt to skate. It was lovely to skate all-round the moat. A super experience.

The grassy banks on top of the Fort made it look like a park. It was possible to play ring tennis (or tenniquoits), a game we played endlessly with a rubber ring, throwing it across a net. It did not take up much space and we could have three or four games going on at the same time. It really kept us fit.

The other thing we used to organise was hikes. We could get ourselves a guard and go off for walks in the countryside, with the guard walking about 20 yards behind us. He did not get in our way and we would stroll wherever we wanted. We had him there so that if anybody, not that anybody did, but if anybody had said, 'Who the hell are you?' or 'What are you doing?,' we could say, 'We have a guard somewhere. Oh, there he is.'

We were marching into the garrison theatre one day, dressed in our best uniforms. Brand-new uniforms, good boots, brasses polished, webbing blancoed. Our little German guards, second rate and totally unfit, wore uniforms from the First World War, with patches in the seats and the knees. They looked really scruffy. We were marching briskly through Thorn, striding out with our guards almost running to keep up with us. A great hulk of a German Hauptman (captain) stepped into the road from the pavement and cried 'Halt!'

PHASE EIGHT

He said, 'What are you doing? You are showing up the German army with your disgusting behaviour.'

We just fell about laughing. We thought it was so funny.

I don't know what he thought we should do, but there we were, young, vigorous, healthy, well-dressed, well-fed men, marching briskly through Thorn. The Poles used to love it. They used to clap as we went past.

The big Forts had things really well organised and did extraordinary things. We went over for the day to one of the Forts. They had a huge festival with funfair shows. I cannot imagine how they did it, but a race without horses was on and we bet on the race. It was a huge operation.

The big Forts, with 2,000–3,000 men in them, had a lot of men to choose from, so they got really top-rate people. We would go to their events. They would come to ours. It meant that during the summer there was a heck of a lot of things going on.

We saw a show at Fort 13 which started with an 'air raid': searchlights shone in the roof of their theatre and revealed an aeroplane which dropped leaflets giving details of the show we were about to see. Sammy Kydd, the TV star, played in their show.

The television company running *This is Your Life* used these photographs as a background to his show.

PHASE NINE

Fort 15 was *non-arbeiters* camp. In the early days it had been used by officers. The reason why British officers were sent to Fort 15 is interesting. No German POWs ever escaped from England although one German POW escaped from Canada. When he got home, in order to curry favour with Hitler, he told terrible stories of how he was treated. So Hitler had the British officers put into Fort 15; because they were officers they had to try to escape. They tried and failed.

What they did do was organise training, lectures and a school. When they were returned to Oflag, in Germany non-allied NCOs took over, senior NCOs.

NCOs, non-commissioned officers – corporals, sergeants, etc. – were meant to be in charge of working parties but there were not enough working parties to go round, so spare NCOs were put into a *non-arbeiters* or non-workers camp, Fort 15 became just such a camp. As well as NCOs, there were medical orderlies who were also non-workers. Fort 15 was full of NCOs and medical orderlies.

I have told you that two men escaped from my room to avoid going back to the Straff (punishment) camp and one lunchtime I was given one hours' notice to leave. I had an hour to load up a trek cart, which I borrowed from Harry, with all my suitcases and clothing, books and everything.

You have no idea what I had, what with the skates and football boots. I put it all on the cart and pushed it off to Fort 15. I was to be there for three months.

PHASE NINE

As soon as I arrived, they found that I was from the hospital so I was put on duty with Jack Cooper, a friend from Fort 14.

They had a chap from the Society of Friends, a very intelligent man, so brilliant that he passed the Institute of Secretaries examination in prison camp. Unfortunately, like many very clever men, he cracked. He was such a nice charming man, a Quaker. He needed two medical orderlies to watch over him night and day. One minute he would be talking to you and the next he would be forcing a fork or knife down his throat. Or he would try to cut his wrist with a knife. We could never relax for a moment.

I was put straight on duty looking after him. I shared a shift with another orderly. We were on four-hour shifts. It was quite a strain. So much so that after a time, which seemed to be for ever, we asked the senior medical officer if the team on duty could be relieved.

There were hundreds of spare medical orderlies in the Fort awaiting repatriation and we thought that someone else should take on the demanding task of watching over this very distressed man.

So at 6 a.m. one morning, Jack Cooper and I handed over our duty to two new orderlies and returned to our room for breakfast. The room, like all the rooms in the Fort, had a window overlooking the dry moat. I had almost finished my breakfast when, suddenly, I saw a man fall past my window. It was the patient we had just left, falling to his death.

The awful sequence of events was this.

After handing over our patient to the two new orderlies they, with the patient, sat down to chat. As I have already said, he was a charming, highly intelligent, irrational man. He very quickly lulled the two new orderlies into a false sense of security. They quickly assumed that we had been fuddy duddies who had exaggerated the seriousness of the case.

'Can we go out and get some fresh air,' he asked them.

'Certainly,' they said and, against every rule that we had laid down, they took him for a walk. Had they restricted the walk to the central platz, where we played cricket, all would have been well. However, he quietly led them up the path which took them to the top of the Fort. The path continued round the Fort and looked like a country walk between the trees.

Chatting away, they continued their walk around the top until the patient threw himself from the top and, by that awful coincidence, he fell past my window.

It was an avoidable tragedy. He suffered terrible injuries and died not long after.

On most days, after my work was over, I was able to join in with all the fantastic activities available. I joined the Fort Rover Scout crew. As there were a lot of Australians who had been captured in Greece and Crete, we played Australian football.

It was like a holiday. It was at Fort 15 that I heard the British news over the radio for the first time. They also had some good records and a portable gramophone. Altogether it was a wonderful rest for me.

In November 1943, the buzz went round that medical orderlies were to be repatriated. Repatriated meant being sent home to England. I was in a quandary. I was a fully trained medical orderly from the hospital. I had been helping with operations and everything. More than that, much more than that, I was one of the 'chosen' twenty-five.

In the First World War there had been a terrifying epidemic of typhus in prison camps. The British authorities feared that the same thing would happen again.

Typhus is carried by lice. The hospital was very short of anti-typhus serum, which came from Canada. They, therefore, gave the injections to one group of twenty-five men in the hospital. The twenty-five formed the nucleus of the hospital with clerks, receptionists and orderlies, and I was one of the medical orderlies chosen. In case there was a big epidemic, we regularly received anti-typhus injections to keep us topped up.

When I first heard about the possibility of repatriation I went to see the senior British officer, Colonel MacKay in Fort 15.

I said, 'I think it would be wrong to send me to England. I am one of the "chosen twenty-five" and I have considerable hospital experience. I am a gunner in the Royal Artillery. If you send me home all I am going to be is a gunner whereas here I am doing a good job. I don't think you should repatriate me. I think you should send me back to Fort 14.'

He agreed with me and arranged for me to return to Fort 14.

He did not tell the Germans. So what was rather interesting was that the week after the repatriation had happened and there was not a single spare medical orderly around, the German Stabsartz came to Fort 14 for his regular weekly check. As he came into my ward he saw me and said, 'I see you are back again,' and smiled. There was not much else he could do really.

PHASE NINE

One splendid idea they had at Fort 15, was that when the meat ration arrived, instead of chopping it up into a mince and putting it in the soup so that it just got lost, they kept it in one piece and roasted it, cooked it as a joint and then carved it up for one room at a time.

So for lunch we only had plain vegetables, but we did not mind because we had got tins of meat in our Red Cross parcels. It did mean, however, that once every three months the room had a roast meal. I had it once in my three months at Fort 15. There were lots of rooms and I think the whole meat ration for the whole of that Fort of thousands of men was one joint of pork.

Boy, oh boy, was it fantastic?

PHASE TEN

When I returned to Fort 14 in November 1943, a new doctor, to replace Mr Cullen, had arrived and a new surgical team had been formed.

They sent me to be an orderly in the 'infectious' hut. I worked with Willy Grant, an RAMC corporal. Very soon after I joined Willy we had a diphtheria epidemic.

I remember one evening, at the height of the epidemic, having patients lined up with their trousers down. As I was sitting in a chair, their bare bottoms were at eye level.

I had a huge syringe, absolutely loaded with about fifty injections of diphtheria serum.

As each of these bottoms passed in front of my eye, whoomp! I injected the whole crowd – whoomp! whoomp! whoomp! That was the diphtheria epidemic.

We also had patients with scarlet fever.

We always had a handful of syphilis cases. Syphilis was difficult to cure in those days. A German scientist had discovered that small quantities of arsenic was the ideal thing to inject them with (Neosalvarsan).

We started off with very small doses and increased the dose gradually. The snag with arsenic is that if it does not get into the vein exactly it causes an ulcer at the site of the injection, so we had to be particularly careful. However, no matter how careful you were, occasionally a drop of arsenic was left behind and the patient developed an ulcer. If we were not very careful we ran out of veins. Sometimes, it meant that we were giving injections into the patient's ankle. We were trying to find a vein anywhere in the patient's body we could use.

PHASE TEN

The bulk of our patients had tuberculosis and mainly they were French. The French did not get Red Cross parcels as we did. They were, therefore, weaker and more prone to catch diseases.

I speak a little French but not all that much. Just enough to try and quieten a man who had haemoptysis. Haemoptysis is where the tubercular lesion breaks into a blood vessel in the lungs and bright frothy blood spews out of the mouth. If you do not watch it fairly carefully, the patient dies just through loss of blood. The only thing you could do, under our circumstances, was to quieten them, to reassure them, to help them to breathe again and in the end, with a bit of luck, the bleeding stops.

I never lost a patient that way, but it was quite a panicky moment when it happened, because you could not panic, that was the point. If you panicked, the patient panicked and they were worse. So you had to reassure them. Trying, in fractured French, to reassure someone who was coughing up blood, spewing all over the floor, was not funny at all.

We had two kinds of patients, open TBs and closed TBs. Open TBs meant that the tuberculosis had broken into the bronchial tubes. They could cough up pus. This meant that the patients were getting better because they were draining the pus out of their lungs. It was highly infectious to anybody around, so we had to be very careful. We were X-rayed frequently to make sure that we had not caught tuberculosis.

The closed TBs, the ones who were really desperately sick with the tuberculosis lesions that had not broken through into the bronchial tubes, and those that were getting better because the pus was draining from their lungs, but were highly infectious to everybody else around, were kept separate from each other.

A friend of mine, Bobby Parkes, had been an orderly looking after the TB patients before me. Unfortunately, he caught TB and died. I was pretty scared for a time when I took over from him; I held my breath for three days.

Willy and I ran this infection ward and, being Willy and me, it was absolutely crazy. We sang all the time with my guitar. We had songs all the evening. It was absolutely riotous because nobody else would come anywhere near us, particularly the Germans. At Appel time the German stood at the bottom of our garden and refused to come any nearer.

I could not do it because I used to laugh, but Willy would march smartly down towards the German, stand about a foot away from him and scream out so loudly that you could hear his voice around the Fort – '*Barrack Drei, vierundzwanzig männer. Zwei sanitater.*' (Barrack Three, twenty-four men. Two sanitators). The German guard would smile, salute, turn around and go back again.

No way would they come anywhere near our hut. No wonder we were the custodians of the radio set!

There was a wonderful atmosphere in the hut. We played petanque or boules. The French played petanque and we played boules. Quite honestly, to these French men it was like a holiday camp. They had been out on severe working parties; been badly fed and they came into this 'Butlins-like' organisation with fun and games and laughter and music and petanque. Morale was fantastic.

The whole of the area of Fort 14 had sandy soil and the atmosphere was very dry. The result was that we had a notable cure rate among the TB cases. Doing nothing except giving them good food, dry air, a relaxed atmosphere, we had some remarkable results. We had men coming in with TB in both lungs and after six months they were almost ready to go home. The Germans accepted that if they had tuberculosis, they should be repatriated.

Willy and I were very pleased because a big batch of French men was sent home. It turned out that one of them, the one who had had a haemoptysis, happened to be the son of the matron of the biggest tuberculosis hospital in Paris. We had a lovely glowing letter, sent through Geneva, congratulating the orderlies and the doctor for all the work they had done and the extremely good condition the men were in. So that was rather nice.

We never lost a man through tuberculosis. We lost lung cancer cases later on, but not tuberculosis.

The doctor we had for our hut was a French doctor, called Lievian. He was a lovely man. He was a real, genuine old-fashioned doctor. He used to listen to their breathing through a little wooden tube-like thing which looked like a tiny trumpet. He would bend down close and listen to their chests.

He would order cupping. Cupping is using little brass pots, rather like egg cups. We would put methylated spirits inside the cup and then we would light it. While the cups were still alight we would clamp them down on the backs of patients, near their lungs. We would first put Vaseline on their backs and, if we were lucky, we did not burn them.

As soon as the cup was slapped on the back of a patient, a vacuum would be created. It would literally suck the skin up into the egg cup-shaped brass pot. The purpose was to relieve congestion.

It is not done today. But it was one of those old-fashioned things that used to be done in the nineteenth century and our French doctor was schooled in the doctorate of that century.

Quite fantastic. He used to amuse us no end by saying, 'And I am very surprise-ed about that' or 'I am amaz-ed.' Anyway, he was a wonderful bloke.

In the French army, their priests are with the men, so we had French priests in our men's POW hospital. In the British army, a priest is an officer and a gentleman, therefore they have to come out from Oflag. That was a strange business because, obviously, it put up a barrier immediately between the priest and the men. Whereas from the French side their priest or pastor was 'one of them'.

If a French soldier, who was a POW, agreed to work for the Germans he could go home. He was repatriated. It says a great deal for the courage of those who stayed behind in the prison camp. They did not succumb to working for the Germans and so missed out on going home to their families.

I had a great deal of time for those French POWs who did not go back to France.

Le Schluuer!

In the First World War, German soldiers were called 'Huns' by the British and 'Bosch' by the French. The 'Hun' is from Attila and his Huns who pillaged and raped their way across Europe.

The German soldiers of the Second World War were aware of the derogatory term and reacted violently if, in their hearing, we called them 'The Hun'.

If someone spoke kindly, then one would call them 'The Gerry' but this did not happen often. Mostly the British called them 'Goons'; – always with the good old British F word preceding 'Goons'.

In the Second World War, the French POWs devised a new name for the Germans. I can only write it phonetically as 'Le Schluuer'; it must be drawn out 'Schchluuuuer …'. The sound gave an impression of somebody who was lower than a snake's belly.

'Le Schchluuuuer ...'

It does not translate, it does not mean anything. It just sounds Schchluuuuer ...

Money

Towards the end of 1943, when I had refused to be repatriated and was sent back to Fort 14, we received letters from the Royal Army Medical Corps people who had been repatriated, saying, 'The army have stopped our pay.'

Let me explain, RAMC personnel, theoretically, were not POWs. They were 'protected' personnel. As such, they were paid by the Germans. In other words, they were still medical orderlies but were working for the 'other' side.

They were paid by the 'other' side. In fact, they should also have received the same rations as the German army. This was because the British army and the German army had signed the Geneva Convention. Therefore, their pay was stopped in England.

These chaps arrived back in England, after four years as a POW, and found they had no money in their account. They were absolutely shattered.

We received a stream of letters saying, 'Do something about it if you can.'

Now it happens that the officers also had their pay at home reduced by the amount they had been paid by the Germany army. Therefore, all the officers in the Oflags had letters back saying, 'You've had your money docked.' In an Oflag everyone was in the same situation and so everybody wanted to try to make money.

The snag was, in their case, nobody went on a working party, nobody earned money, except what they were paid by the Germans. They found themselves in a very difficult position. In fact, many of them returned home after five years as a POW and found that they had not got anywhere near the money they had expected and hoped for.

I looked at this situation and thought, 'Well now, I am in the Royal Artillery, it is possible that I have not had my pay docked. Nobody in my unit had entered into my pay book that I was a stretcher bearer.'

PHASE TEN

I have said previously that as soon as I got to prison camp somebody wrote it in for me so that I could say to the Germans 'I am a registered stretcher bearer.'

The point was that I was not sure what the British army thought about this.

I worked out how much money may have been docked from my pay. In terms of cash, it was £180. I thought, well, fine. I have got to earn that money.

The Germans accepted that there was a problem and they made an arrangement that if one paid money into Stalag they would acknowledge receipt of it and would transfer the money via Geneva back to England to one's home address. So, I wrote to my dad and told him what was happening.

I decided that as a medical orderly there was only one way I could 'earn' money and that was to win it at cards.

Nobody else in my ward was in the same position as me. They had not had their pay docked. They were all out on working parties, they were absolutely swimming in money.

The money we had was called 'lagergeld' – German camp money. So far as the boys in my ward were concerned, it was *Monopoly* money. They could not buy anything with it in the camp canteen except toothpaste and silly things like that – anything else we purchased was 'bought' with Red Cross produce – like soap and cigarettes. Cigarettes were the currency, not lagergeld.

I got down seriously playing cards. I did not cheat; I am good at playing cards. I played solo whist and I won, over a period of two or three months, £180. I sent it home to Dad and as soon as I had won the amount of money I needed I stopped playing cards.

Suffice it to say, that when I did get home and looked up my pay book, I found that the army had not docked any money. Therefore, I had received all my normal money from the army.

The amount of money that I had sent home, through winning at cards, was the down payment of No 6 Peploe Road, Willesden, London. The first house that my wife, Trudy, and I bought for £1,300 in 1945.

Gardens

I have previously stated that we did not have apples. We could not grow apple trees, it takes too long. However, what we did have was gardens.

At the end of each barrack, the medical orderlies had their own vegetable garden. As we were permanent staff we could establish ourselves; we bought seeds and each spring we planted spring onions, lettuce and carrots, the sort of general stuff you can grow easily and quickly, particularly the onions, because that was something that really was a delicacy to add to our corned beef.

I enjoyed tending our vegetable gardens; it was quite good fun and we would gain great benefit in the autumn when we harvested our crop. It was quite nice, like the vegetable patch at the bottom of the garden. Although it was not very big, because we did not have all that much space, it was enough to satisfy our needs.

We also made a seat by the side of the moat. It was just like sitting beside a river – it really was super.

The Russians

Since 1941, we had had thousands of Russians in camps in Thorn. The Russian camps were organised by the Russians themselves; the Germans never went into the Russian camps because they knew they would be lynched. However, in 1944 the Germans panicked because they thought they were going to have a typhoid epidemic on their hands in the Russian camps.

We had a request from the German Stabsartz: would we be prepared to send a big team of doctors and medical orderlies to the Russian POW camp in Thorn and inject all 5,000 men with anti-typhoid vaccinations? Could we please organise the teams and do it?

We said, 'Yes, of course.'

I was in one of the teams who walked over to the Russian camp. It was unbelievable. The German guards opened the outside gates, pushed us in and closed the gates hard. No German guard entered the camp at all.

We walked gingerly into this camp of 5,000 Russian men and were greeted at the inner gate by a Russian guard who took us to his commandant. We explained what we had been asked to do.

The Russians we see on the television, mostly from Moscow and St Petersburg, look like Europeans. This is because the 'Rus' are blonde, blue-eyed people who came from Scandinavia. These same 'Vikings', who also occupied Normandy, Britain and Ireland, occupied parts of Russia with the result that those 'Russians', the ones we see, look like Europeans.

However, Russia is not European at all, it is Asiatic, and this was my first experience of Asiatic Russians en masse. I was stunned. There was just a handful of 'European' Russians. All the rest of the 5,000 were little, squat, stubby, high cheek-boned, squat-nosed Mongolians (Tartars). When the Tartars swept across Russia from Siberia they left their progeny behind, meaning that outside of Moscow and St Petersburg many people are of Mongolian descent.

The European Russians – big, tall lads, as distinct from the little squat Mongolians, carried big sticks with which they would go into a hut and beat everybody out, beat them into three lines and through the camp to march up to where we were standing.

We had five teams – it was like five check-out counters at a supermarket – each team did 1,000 injections. Our system was simple but efficient. Somebody was hit over the back and driven up to where an orderly would clean an arm with alcohol. The next orderly gave the jabs, the next cleaned it again with alcohol and – whoomp – with a stick the Russian would be beaten back into line again. They were worse than animals.

I was absolutely stunned. If I had not been there and seen it with my own eyes, I would not have believed it.

Wowee! They were serfs. I suppose that was it. It was still the old 'Tsarist/serf concept'. It was an interesting experience.

In 1966, in Oxford, I taught Russian students marketing!!

PHASE ELEVEN

In August 1944, we moved to 'Kopernikus Lager'. Kopernicus (Copernicus) lived in Thorn in 1543. He first evolved the theory that the sun did not go round the earth but that the earth went round the sun. It was not until about 100 years later that everybody agreed with him. Thorn has a statue to Kopernicus.

In the late summer of 1944, the Germans suddenly closed Fort 14 down. They wanted it for their own use and we were all shifted to Kopernicus Lager.

Kopernicus Lager was like the kind of prison camp that you saw pictures of, with barbed wire all the way round. It was just sand. No greenery at all; it was absolutely dreadful. It had been used by the RAF and as the RAF had to escape there was every kind of treble, quadruple, barbed wire. It did not worry us because we were not going to escape, but it was a depressing, ghastly place.

The first morning, Willy and I were taken down in a lorry with our bedding to begin to prepare our barrack for our patients. As I stepped off the tail-board of the lorry, I was almost sick; the fleas came up off the sand as high as my waist. It was really foul.

For the last few years we had been able to keep ourselves clean. We did not have any lice. Now, suddenly, we had fleas. In fact, it was so bad that Willy and I had to sleep on tables to keep us out of their reach. However, it seemed that they could only jump up to about waist height, so Willy and I got buckets of Lysol and sprayed and scrubbed out the whole of the barracks, so apart from that first day, we were rid of them. I cannot tell you what it was like to have all these fleas up to your waist.

Willy and I had a big barrack for our infectious cases. Our own room was rather pleasant. It was quite a big room at the end of the barrack, split into two sections. The first half we used as our surgery with all our drugs and everything, the second half was our living quarters.

It was a huge camp so that we had our own football pitch in the middle of the camp. So that was not bad; we made it all right.

What was interesting was the entertainment theatre.

Because the RAF, the previous tenants, had been trying to escape, they had taken away the rafters from the theatre hut to support their tunnel. You could see the roof sag, so it was not safe to use as our theatre because it was just unsafe. So we got ourselves organised and used another room as our entertainment theatre.

Nearly caught!

This was the camp where Willy and I had our nearest escapade with the Germans.

I have explained how the Germans came one night and I picked up the suitcase with the radio in it and put it behind the man who was to die a couple of days later from lung cancer. Because we were the custodians of the radio, we used to invite about half a dozen other members of the hospital staff to listen to the radio each evening. By 9 o'clock there were usually half a dozen men in our room ready to listen to the radio. The radio was packed into a suitcase which was opened on the table. The wire was pushed into the electric light plug. We put the earphones in a bowl so that we could all hear the news, and we were in business. It was marvellous for these lads to listen to news from home. We, of course, heard it every night.

That night we had not been warned. Suddenly, I heard a scuffling in the outer room, the one we used for our drugs. I rushed to the door and stood in the doorway.

Two German guards were searching; they were looking in the cupboards and through everything. They just pushed me aside but, fortunately, my standing in the doorway had blocked their view, giving the fellows who had been sitting round the table time to jump to their feet and stand to one side. The radio operator, with presence of mind, had pulled the plug out, pushed the wire into the suitcase and closed the suitcase.

These two Germans then walked into our living room. They dragged the suitcases out from under our beds and looked into them. They dragged suitcases out from the cupboards and looked at them, but they did not touch the suitcase on the table.

Wow! We died a million deaths.

But there it was – we got away with it – again!

The bath house

We did not have a bath house in the camp as we had had at Fort 14. The result being that each week we had to be marched down to a communal bath house the way they do it in the army.

Whether it is the British army or the German army, it seems to be the same. You go in, strip off, stand under the shower and somebody says 'Go!' They switch the water on and you get wet. They switch the water off so you can soap yourself and then they switch it on again so you can slosh yourself down. Everybody has to jump at the same time.

It worked, so that was that.

A great sight

The end of the war was nigh, and a very obvious sign came one afternoon.

We could hear the deep drone of aircraft engines and, looking up, there was a great sight in the sky. It seemed like hundreds of American aircraft circling overhead. As we watched it, it became apparent what was happening just above us.

The escorting fighter aeroplanes, the twin-boomed 'Lightnings' were returning straight home to England before their fuel ran out, to be replaced by 'Mustangs' who were to escort the bombers home.

What a sight!

What a morale boost for us!

What a disaster for our German guards!

PHASE ELEVEN

What a memory!

Harry Morice had the most extraordinary memory.

We all had pyjamas, striped pyjamas, all different colours. Harry was remarkable, I always used to forget what colour my pyjamas were, but Harry always knew.

You took the pyjamas down to Harry to get washed and he sent them back out.

As I have said, he had Polish women to wash our laundry. Harry knew which were your pyjamas. He knew everyone's pyjamas. Quite an extraordinary, wonderful fellow.

A drop in our morale

Kopernicus Lager was just outside Thorn on the south bank of the Vistula River towards the west. We had quite a long road to walk into town. This meant that we walked past Polish houses, hovels really. The standard of living of the Poles, at that time, was very low. The Germans treated them as second-class citizens. The Germans called us 'Tommy' and treated us as equals.

Until just before Christmas 1944 we thought we were winning the war, what with D-Day and all the excitement of our army sweeping across France into Belgium. But on 16 December the Battle of the Bulge started. The Germans used forty tank divisions to drive towards Antwerp to try to cut off the British Expeditionary Force from the Americans. If they had succeeded, they would have held back the war for a long time – and for a few days it looked as though their gamble would come off. But it did not. When the weather improved and our air force could get into the air, we hammered the German tanks.

I can assure you, that as POWs in Kopernikus Lager, thinking that the war was almost over, our hearts sank to hear about the Battle of the Bulge. The morale of the camp just plummeted. I remember it because I had gone into Thorn to go to the hospital, which is where we heard the news, and we thought, 'Won't it ever end?'

Let's face it, when you are in your twenties, five years as a POW is a long time. I cannot tell you how our morale sank.

'Infected' at a critical time

While I was in Dresden in January 1945, I had a bit of a problem with my right hand. What had happened was that I had somehow got an infection in it. I had been nursing a Frenchman who had caught scarlet fever and for some time I worried that I had caught an infection from him.

Whilst I was on this trip to Dresden, the infection got worse and worse so that when I returned to Fort 14 the doctors had to operate on me, open up my hand and drain the pus away. So my arm was in a sling at a critical time.

We had been listening to the news and we knew that, at last, the Russians had broken through at Warsaw. They had waited until the Germans had wiped out the Polish resistance, because the last thing that Stalin wanted was a Polish resistance. On 11 January, the Russians entered Warsaw and we knew that this was the end.

Now, interestingly enough, during the whole time we had been POWs we had never conceived that we would have to WALK anywhere. In fact, even at that stage, we did not think that we were going to have to WALK home.

Just picture what it is like as a POW in Poland, thinking 'How we are going to get back to Britain?' We thought we might get a train to Danzig and come home by steamer through the Baltic. Sometimes, we wondered about parachute troops dropping to release us. We had no idea.

The least idea of all was that we would be released by the Russians. That was something we had never dreamed of, but now the time was approaching when the Russians were going to come to us.

Fortunately for me, my great friend, Harry Morice, had said to me 'Vic, I think we should be ready for any eventuality.' I agreed with him.

So he organised it. He got me and himself a nice big rucksack, a water bottle, a haversack and boots with a double sole. We packed a blanket, spare underclothes and socks, and concentrated food like Horlicks tablets.

PHASE TWELVE

In January 1945, the Red Army began to advance again. We heard this on the radio. The Red Army was advancing from Warsaw, and Russian bombers came screaming over the camp on their way to bomb the bridges over the Vistula River.

The German guards gave us an hour's notice to move off.

The reason we had to move ahead of the Russian army was because the Germans wanted to keep us as hostages. The plan of the OKW (the Oberkommando der Wehrmacht, the general Staff of the German army) was to finally make a stand in the Austrian Redoubt. They had seen how the Swiss had made use of the mountains to defend themselves and they thought they could do the same. They needed British and American POWs in the Redoubt to stop the Allies from dropping the atom bomb.

Had they made it, defended by SS troops, it would have created a problem for the Allies. Fortunately, Patton's army took over the area before the Germans. So the plan came to nought. Thank goodness!

The march

Because I had my arm in a sling and because the doctors thought that we were all going to get on a railway train, they said to me, 'We think there is going to be a battle in Thorn.' They thought that the hospital would be used for casualties. It was not, but they were not to know that at the time.

'As you have your arm in a sling, you won't be much use as a medical orderly, therefore, you had better go on a train.' I had other ideas.

A mate of mind had built himself a sledge for that winter. In Kopernicus Lager there was a slope and some of the fellows had quite enjoyed themselves with a sledge.

So I said to him, 'Right ho, mate, you're going to stay behind, but I want your sledge.' So we made a deal and I had a sledge.

I went to Harry and said, 'Look here is my sledge with my rucksack, haversack and water bottle. I've got my pair of special boots on and my overcoat. What else have you got for me?' Harry piled the sledge with Red Cross parcels and gave me a medical pannier. In fact, it was two white sacks filled with medical equipment.

So that by towing with my left hand, I had a sledge with a haversack, water bottle, rucksack, Red Cross parcels and a medical panier and off I went.

As we all streamed out of the camp, with spare staff and patients who could walk, we met a stream of men coming down from Einheit Drei. They thought they were going on a train. Chaps were carrying piano accordions and guitars. One bloke was actually carrying a double bass. Can you just picture that, a double bass! Some carried suitcases absolutely laden with stuff.

Off we went – but not to the station. I should think not, considering the state the German army was in at that moment, there were no spare trains for POWs. We turned sharp left out of the camp and marched west towards Bromberg.

The date was 20 January, the depth of the winter in Poland, with snow thick on the ground and frozen roads. In fact, the only way the Poles moved around in the winter was to take the wheels off their carts and put skis on. Their horses and carts became horse-drawn sledges with bells in a figure U over the top of them. It was quite pretty.

But this was the situation, the weather situation. It was fine for a sledge; with hard ice on the roads, the sledge ran very well. But you can imagine how soon the sides of the road became strewn with clothes that had been thrown out of the suitcases. The chap with the double bass had tied a bit of string round it and was towing it along the road, along the ice. It was not long before it fell apart.

It was frightful, absolutely shambolic. When dusk came, at about half past four, they just turned us right into afield which led down to the River Vistula.

PHASE TWELVE

So just picture a huge 20-acre field with thousands of POWs pushed into it. The snow was about 3ft deep and an ice-frozen river was at the bottom of the field. In the distance we could hear the guns, bombs and machine guns. By then the Red Army was approaching fast on the other side of Thorn.

Though we were told not to, we lit fires to try to warm ourselves, so just picture this scene: a vast field with groups of figures on it, all huddled together to try to keep warm, with a fire blazing if they could. There is only one thing to do to sleep under those circumstances and that is to group as closely as you can together. Whatever blankets or overcoats you have got split them in half, half go on the ground, because most of the cold comes up from below, then lie as closely together as possible and place the other half of the blankets and overcoats on top. You did not dare to take your boots off, otherwise they and your feet would freeze.

We were a bit silly because we were not really experienced in this kind of thing, but we subsequently found out what the Russians do.

If twenty-five men lie down with their shoulders touching, their feet in the middle, it makes a complete circle, because your shoulders are wide, your feet are quite narrow and as long as your shoulders are touching you get warmth from each person. It is the real way to sleep out in those conditions. A lot of men gave up there and then. There was no way they could carry on. It really caught them out terribly. Frozen, absolutely frozen all night. By the time we got to Bromberg, a lot of men had dropped out with pneumonia etc.

Although the Russians were, ostensibly, our allies, I do not think there were many of us wanting to be released by the Russians. They were 'trigger happy' and we could not speak their language.

The men in hospital who stayed behind were not very happy about it either but, as they were non-combatant, they thought they could get away with it and they did. I heard, when I eventually arrived home, that they had had some tricky moments.

It was not only the Russians who worried us but also the Germans who were 'cleaning up' after themselves. If anybody was left behind they were either shot by the SS or shot by the front-line Russian troops as they came through. In a front line everybody is trigger happy, very trigger happy and you can never guarantee that you are going to pass successfully through a front line, particularly when you are not very good at speaking Russian.

At that time, there were two Russian armies. One from the south and one going north into East Prussia. What the Germans decided to do with us was to try to march between the Russian armies, which meant that we were making for Bromberg. We were then turned north-west towards the Baltic.

The Russians too were making for the Baltic. I have a very vivid picture in my mind of walking along a road, with Russian tanks on either side of us in the fields.

I also clearly remember getting up one morning to find that the road had been shot up. There were dead civilians and horses on the road because the Polish civilians were fleeing before the Russian advance. It was something which the Germans tried to stop. In fact, later on they did stop people leaving their towns because they did not want the roads cluttered up with refugees. They wanted free movement for their troops. They had seen how refugees had slowed down our army in Belgium in 1940 and did not want it to happen to them.

It was a great shambles; it was a sort of nightmare really.

I know that, somehow, I got away from the rest of the column with another fellow with a sledge. By an extraordinary coincidence, I met him in Covent Garden Market after the war. He was selling Australian fruit and he and chatted for quite a while about the march. This chap with a mate and a sledge. Me with my mate, John Fawcett, and a sledge.

The four of us started branching out on our own. I do not know what we thought we were going to try and do. One night we went into a big house where we found many other refugees already sheltering. They did not argue with us at all. Nobody said anything. We just kipped down on the floor in one of the big rooms.

During the night, the door burst open and standing there were soldiers in German army uniform. They were, in fact, Latvian Waffen SS troops. What had happened was that whilst we were asleep, the Russians had occupied that area. The Latvians had pushed them back and these men just burst into this room to make sure that there were no Russians in there.

One of the Polish refugees looked up and explained what the situation was so they went off and left us to get to sleep again. And that was it.

The next morning when we go up, we found the road absolutely strewn with dead horses and people. What a bloody mess.

The four of us caught a fright and thought we had better go and join the column again. We found out where it was and when we got to the little township that evening, true enough, there was our column. They had all been shepherded into a church.

PHASE TWELVE

I did not like the idea of kipping down in a church, so we wandered down the road and found a barn. There was straw and it was warm.

By about this time we had begun to run out of our Red Cross food. We had eaten our tins and everything. I know this does not sound possible, but, unbelievably somebody came to where we were, upstairs in this barn, and said, 'Do you know what we've found down below? We've found it is full of American Red Cross parcels.'

Apparently, American soldiers must have been staying there and they had just left this huge supply of Red Cross parcels. So we went down and opened up all the parcels and took out all the things, like meat and cheese, as much as we could carry. We filled our rucksacks and sledges. In those early days of the march, we were not getting any food from the Germans at all.

The fellows who had not brought any food with them, who had walked out of the camp carrying suitcases were, by this time, in a sorry state. We were losing a lot of men. They were just falling by the wayside.

Constantly, we heard the Russian guns. It took a month to reach the River Oder on about 20 February, so that in the whole of that month, never once were we out of the sound of the Russian guns.

Another time, we had been pushed into what had previously been a big German barracks. At 2 o'clock in the morning, the Russian guns sounded very near. There was a great scream from the Germans and we were put back on the march again. It was panic stations. The Russians were at one end of the village as we fled from the other end.

There was a strange incident for me. I was very tired; I was not feeling too good, pulling my sledge. The German sergeant who had been in charge of our camp was also on the march. He saw the state I was in and he pulled my sledge all that night. I gave him cigarettes and that was that!!

Another picture I have in my mind is of a blizzard blowing horizontally across a snow-clad field with me marching at the head of the column. As we marched across the field, we saw bodies lying on either side of the path. Ahead of us was a Russian column and as the Russians collapsed they were left on the side, freezing to death. We marched past. What else could we do? It was all we could do to take ourselves, let alone take anybody else.

But, I promise you, talk about walking past on the other side. Maybe the good Samaritan was fortunate that he was well fed and had money in his pocket so that he could pay for the man to go to an inn. There was no way we could do that with these poor Russians.

An episode in the snow

We were very weak. It was so cold with blizzards. I cannot imagine how we kept going. I really do not know. I was feeling very low.

One day we had marched and marched and marched and suddenly, in front of us was a great hill. Down the hill and then up the hill; it was a terrible struggle, pulling our sledge.

When we got to the top, the German said, 'I am very sorry. I have made a mistake, we have come too far. We have got to go back again.' I nearly did not make it that night.

The whole tension, the whole atmosphere was awful on that march. We were cold and hungry and we did not know what was going on. The Russians were all around us in that first month and it was frightful.

The Germans were desperate to try to establish a line in Pomerania for the battle for Küstrin.

We marched past a little strip of hills. It was very pleasant. A tourist spot normally, but these hills could now become a good defence barrier. The SS were stationed across the road, stopping any soldier and directing them into this line. It did not matter what you were, what rank you were, you were diverted to join this line. A last-ditch stand.

They moaned like anything, letting all these POWs go through with their guards. The guards had a hell of a job trying to stay with us, otherwise they would have been kept behind to hold the line.

We marched on to the River Oder and went on a ferry boat across the big wide harbour. There was a lot of German shipping in the harbour. It was a strange feeling really.

Once we were across the other side of the river, for the first time, we were out of hearing of the Russian guns.

It was coming up to spring. The snow was disappearing and we had to do something else for transport. So me, being me, we DID do something else. That something else was to get hold of a four-wheeled cart, which is very common in Poland.

I transferred my food, rucksack and everything from the sledge onto the cart. From a sledge to a cart. Later somebody pinched it and I got a pram! Well you had to have something.

The refugees. Imagine how you would feel if you were a Pole living in a village due to be overrun by the Red Army. What would you do, particularly if you had women with you? Answer – you would run away. We saw refugees for the first time, in France and Belgium in 1940, but at least it was summer time then.

In 1945, in the early part of March, it was winter with deep snow, blizzards, ice and fog, not the fog of war, but an icy fog. If you were foolish enough to take your boots off at night, they froze solid and you could not get them on again.

All this and now homeless. At the start of their journey, most of these farming Poles had a horse and cart. Townspeople were just not allowed to leave because they would clutter up the roads for the army. Certainly, as soon as the Russians reached Germany proper, their civilians were not allowed to get onto the roads. Their horses were soon taken from them by the German army. All they could do then was to try to find hand carts and to pile everything they could on the carts and go west.

Grandma sat on top. She was the one I was called to try to help when her toes were frostbitten. Sad to say there was absolutely nothing I could do other than to give the family some ointment to rub into Grandma's toes!

Like us, the refugees were kept off the roads and out of the towns. The only town we walked through was Schwerin and that was for propaganda purposes.

The Germans had learnt the lessons of France where the British and French armies were delayed in 1940 by refugees. It was not going to happen to them in 1945. The plight of these refugees was frightful. They, unlike us, had women and children to contend with. It was horrendous!

Eventually, millions moved west and helped to rebuild West Germany. They helped the German miracle of redevelopment after the war.

The reason why the 'wall' was built to stop them.

Getting organised

Once we got over the River Oder we got things organised. First of all, we made a list of all the men on the march. Until then we did not know how many chaps we had with us. When we had started out from Thorn we must have had about 3,000, comprised of men from all of the Forts. By that time, we only had 700 left. We had lost these men in that first month. We now had the names and numbers of all the chaps remaining.

This is where I was issued with my *Ausweis*, my pass, which allowed me to go around doing medical work each evening. We got things quite well organised. We would march for three days and then rest for a day, march for three days and then rest.

I found out later that this was the system of marching used by the Tsars to take prisoners to Siberia. In their case, they marched 3,000 miles in nine months. We did 1,000 in three months.

As we slowly began to get organised, so the Germans also got themselves organised.

We were in one of the parts of Germany where they grow lots of potatoes. What the Germans did was to send one of their men on ahead, on his bicycle and find farms with big barns.

We would be split up into groups of 200–300 and go into these huge barns. The German officer in charge would make arrangements with the farmers to steam potatoes. True they were not washed, they were all with the dirt and everything else, but at least they would steam them – 'Pig' potatoes they were called.

As we went into the barn that evening, we would each take our cap off and get steamed potato put into it. At least it was something. It was better than nothing. If, like me, you still had some Red Cross food, well then it was a good supplement. A bit of cheese on hot potato is not too bad. At least it keeps you going.

The Map

At about this time I was given a map by one of the men on the march. For a POW to have a map of Germany was *'Streng Verboten'*, strictly forbidden. The Germans considered that a map was an aid to escape. At this moment in the war, no one on our column wanted to escape. We had strength in numbers. We were walking west. We would not get along any more quickly or safely on our own.

So, because I was in the organising hierarchy, one of the lads thought that I could make good use of this map, so I marked out our route as carefully as I could. From Thorn up to the Baltic in the snow and blizzards was so confusing I just guessed it.

We crossed the Oder at Swinemünde, just south of Peenemünde where they built the V weapons until, one night the RAF bombed it to smithereens. From there, we moved west past, not into, Anklam, Jarmen, Demmin,

Teterow, Güstrow to Schwerin. We then marched south-west, passing Hamburg (30-odd miles away), past Hagenow until we crossed the Elbe, via a broken bridge, to Uelzen and then Celle where we caught the train south to Hamelin on the River Weser, then east back towards the Russians and ahead of the advancing Americans, south of Hildesheim, Salzgitter and finally to Ummendorf where we were released by the Americans. One thousand miles in three months!

One of the guards saw me looking at my map and demanded that I hand it over to him. He had a gun, so I did. However, I was not going to stand for that, particularly at this stage in the war, so I spoke to the British commandant, a wonderful CQMS called Grainger, truly a man who it was a privilege to know. He agreed that I should have the map and made the guard return it to me. I still have it as a treasured possession.

Carry on, carrying on

We did about 15 miles a day for three days and rested up for a day. But with all these potatoes, bad water and any raw vegetables we could find, the men started getting dysentery. It just squirted out of us. As I was the only sanitator from the hospital, I was the senior medic on the column; I was the only one who really knew what needed doing.

So I marched at the head of the column. As we went through a village I would stop off at a chemist shop, buy up as much medication as I could and then rejoin the column as it went through. Each evening I would use my medical equipment. I would walk round to each of the barns looking at blisters and ulcers. Sometimes, of course, chaps had been beaten over the head with a rifle butt. It was all a nightmare.

I remember on one occasion I caught dysentery and was so weak that my mate, John Fawcett, literally carried me to the barn that night. Thank God it was a night where we stayed for a whole day of rest and so I managed to pull myself together to continue on the march.

This was where we started to have to leave men behind. A group of twenty or thirty who just could not go on. We started a system which kept us going for quite a time. We would say to the farmer, 'We have plenty of money, we will pay for you to have your horse and cart to follow behind the column to pick up men who fall out on the wayside.'

We did not want to leave our men to die by the roadside like the Russians did. The trouble with this system is that you always find swine, in any situation, who try to exploit the system; I had to be very careful that the men who were on the horse and cart were men who really could not march.

Because I had to march all day, work all evening doing my rounds, I put my kit on the cart. We had about ten men on the cart to start with. We would pick as few up as we could on the way. But you always got the scroungers – I remember vividly one or two occasions. I would see a chap lying by the side of the road groaning away and would have a pretty good idea that he was a shyster. I would kick him hard and say, 'Go on.' He would say, 'Oh you bastard!' but then just walk on; he was just trying to swing the lead to get a lift in the horse and cart.

The reason it was necessary to be ruthless came home to me later on the march. The day before we were released – we did not know that that was to be, of course – Allan Periman, a very, very clever man who I knew well as he had worked in the library in Stalag, said to me, 'Vic, I know you are under tremendous pressure, but please may I go on the cart today?'

I said, 'Oh Allan, I wish you had told me before. Of course, you can old chum, you are not a scrounger.'

Unfortunately, he had left it too late. I went to the German sergeant and said, 'We are going to have another man die today.' Allan died that afternoon. We were released the next day.

So no wonder I was harsh on the shysters because obviously every space on that horse and cart was valuable.

It is worth noting that I was also called in to help with the refugees who also walked with us. The Germans too requested my help with their blisters. On one occasion, a Russian POW asked me to remove a torn fingernail, which I did, and without a single murmur from the Russian – a real tough guy.

My set of instruments

I was given a set of instruments packed into a metal case 80mm x 150mm x 20mm deep. I am looking at it as I write. It consists of scissors, a fold-away scalpel, a cut-throat razor, a pair of Spencer-Wells forceps, for gripping and holding an artery, a probe, an aneurysm needle, for sliding under an artery prior to tying it off, one pair of conventional forceps and three pairs of forceps with a clip which allows them to act as a pair of Spencer-Wells forceps. They were very, very useful in many ways.

My most interesting use of them happened just a few days before we were released by the Americans, though as I have said we did not know that at the time.

One of the German Unteroffiziers had noticed one of our chaps' mortal distress. The man in question had never reported sick. I was, therefore, unaware of his plight. He had somehow developed an infection of his neck which had resulted in pus forming to such an extent that, in ballooning up in such quantity, it had made his breathing difficult.

I had him put on the horse and cart and arranged with the Unteroffizier to make arrangements for me to have, that evening, a clean table with lots of hot water, in a farm house. This he did during the day. I bought a local anaesthetic in a glass spray from an Apotek and, with John Fawcett's help, I froze the chap's neck in the place I had chosen and, using the scalpel, I opened up his neck and inserted the forceps. I had an enamel kidney dish handy to catch the cupful of pus which poured out.

It relieved his condition immediately and we were able, a few days later, to hand him over to an American doctor. The man himself was as pleased as punch and the Unteroffizier thought I was a miracle man to cut a man's throat without killing him!

We finally arrived in Schwerin

Schwerin has a lake and was quite pleasant. They paraded us through the streets; the streets were lined with Germans, but do not forget that they were beaten. Here we were POWs. We had been taken as POWs in 1940, but they did not know that and here were POWs being paraded through the streets to try to boost their morale.

One of our blokes, in front of all these women who were all lining the streets, took his trousers down and did his business all over the road. All squelching all over the road and I thought that was lovely. Up yours!!

Two Hitler Youth boys were pointing at us and jeering. There was an old Prussian, iron-grey hair, short crop, you know the kind, and he kicked their arse and said, 'How dare you, they are soldiers. It does not matter that they are POWs. They are soldiers, how dare you jeer at them.'

Funny isn't it?

The next step on our march was crossing the River Elbe on a bridge which had been blown up by bombs. It was a difficult job getting across, but, slowly but surely, we crossed the Elbe and started to make our way to Celle across the Lüneburger Heide (Lüneburg Heath). Our morale was sky high. It was enjoyable – a lovely spring hike across a beautiful part of Germany.

Washing weakens one!

At about this time of the march we began to get organised enough for a bunch of us to arrange for hot water to be available for a good wash down. For the first time in I suppose seven or eight weeks, I took off my clothes. I sponged myself down with this hot water and nearly fainted. I felt as weak as a kitten.

Astonishing really. Thank goodness it was a rest day. I had to lie down afterwards to recover.

Bombing Hamburg

The Lüneburg Heath is quite near Hamburg. I remember on that spring morning watching a bombing raid on Hamburg. I was leaning against a tree, looking up into the crystal clear sky. I could see a group of twenty-five American planes and then a few miles behind another group of twenty-five and behind them another group. I could see them right into the distance, those groups of twenty-five – I suppose there were about ten groups all together.

The way the Americans operated, at that time of the war, was when the senior bomb aimer pressed the bomb-release button, everybody pressed their button too and it was 'bombs away!'

Twenty-five planes, 10 tons of bombs on each plane, 250 tons of bombs as a group, all dropped in unison. When that lot hit the deck, it was like a minor atomic explosion. The whole earth trembled. What it must have been like underneath I cannot imagine; it was bad enough for us and we were miles away. It was unbelievable. The war had reached the stage where the conventional bombs were simulating the power of an atomic weapon, without the radiation.

PHASE TWELVE

In the end, we eventually did catch a train at Celle to Hamelin on the River Weser.

We were in the railway siding of Hildesheim after it was bombed. American bombers came over in an intense bombing raid that wiped out 83 per cent of the houses in that town – a town about the size of Oxford. That must have been 23 March 1945, the war was almost over, but somebody decided that there was a town in front of the American army that had never been bombed before, and so 83 per cent was destroyed in one raid. This business of simulating atom bombs was quite true.

At this stage we split up into three groups.

Hamelin (or Hamlyn)

When we arrived at Hamelin in the early morning, after an all-night march, I thought I had better see if I could get some food for our group of 200 men; I thought that there must be a Red Cross place in the town. So off I went with my cart and a couple of fellows to help me. Because I had an *Ausweis* nobody was going to trouble me, and nobody did.

We found a French camp in town and carried back quite a lot of food by piling it on the cart and towing it back.

I made a distribution to our men. It was a help for the fellows. They had been put into what had been a sugar factory. Some of the boys had climbed into the big boilers and scraped out sugar, so they were stuffing themselves with sugar, burnt sugar, from the walls of these cookers.

I thought I had better get more medical equipment and so went off to a chemist in the village. We were just outside Hamelin. I had bought the medicine and just begun to walk back when I heard a noise. I looked up and there, immediately above me, was a great American bomber. A Liberator bomber. Just, literally, sweeping over the village to bomb it, or so I thought.

I was absolutely stunned to see this bomber and for a split second, I thought, 'Oh, blimey, five years of POW life, come all this way, to be bombed by your own people seemed a bit hard. Well I had better go into an air-raid shelter.' Believe me, it was a strange feeling. I walked down into a civilian air-raid shelter with the German civilians from the village, sheltering from the air raid. They looked at me and I looked at them but nobody said a word. It was a very funny business to be in a German airraid shelter sheltering from the American bombers with a lot of German civilians.

In fact, the plane was about to crash land, and crash land it did, in the field.

But that day the Americans dive-bombed the railway station. At that moment, stopped in the station were a couple of German Red Cross trains with red crosses on the top.

If you want to block a railway line there is no better way than to zap trains in the station. The American dive-bombers came over and zap, zap, zapped these Red Cross trains in the station. Nobody is clean in war.

That evening, as I went back to the sugar factory, hoping to get a good night's sleep, they put us on the march again. So off we went. I had marched a day and then a night to get to Hamelin. I spent the day in Hamelin getting food and medicine and now I was marching all night. I was like a zombie. Absolutely like a zombie. I can truthfully say that I have never been so tired in my life. I was literally sleep walking. No question at all, it was absolutely dreadful. But there it was.

This time we were actually marching AWAY from the Americans, TOWARDS the Russians.

The American 9th Army catches up with us

I now realise why they marched us at night. It was safer. As dawn broke, they pushed us into a barn and, like zombies, we just passed out.

The Americans were strafing the roads with machine guns and cannons. I remember sitting up, trembling with fear. I seemed to be the only man awake in this barn of 200 men. Overhead flew a stream of American Tomahawks, single-seater fighter bombers. They screamed overhead.

Immediately over our barn, they opened fire. They were shooting up the road which was just by the side of the barn. Thank God somebody did not open up just too soon, otherwise they would have just ripped our barn apart.

There was nothing we could do. We were in this flimsy barn with all these planes zooming around immediately over the top of the barn, opening up with their machine guns and cannons.

PHASE TWELVE

Blimey, was I scared! When they say you 'tremble with fright', you really do, you really do tremble and your teeth chatter.

We kept marching for about a week south of Brunswick. I can remember looking up into the sky one day to see four American B17 Flying Fortresses flying in formation. Then the Germans opened up with their anti-aircraft guns. One of the B17s just disappeared.

You cannot believe it, there you were looking up to the sky at four of them and suddenly there were only three and a few parachutes coming down.

We heard later from the American army how lucky we were not to get killed. We were shambling along the road in a gaggle. Apparently, the American tanks had us line up with their guns and were going to blow us out of the road. Somebody said, 'No, they are wearing khaki, maybe they are POWs.' Then someone else said, 'We won't zap them,' and they did not zap us.

PHASE THIRTEEN

11 April 1945 – Being released

That night as we finally reached a small town called Ummendorf we found a barn. The German sergeant called Thompson, an Australian in charge of our group and myself and said, 'We are going to leave you now. We are going to try and make a break. So goodbye.' And off they went. Thompson was a very smart Australian sergeant. He really knew what he was about.

We chose some solid lads and put them on guard on our own fellows because we knew that if we had let these lads loose they would have gone into the village and the likelihood was that they would be shot up by the SS. So we had to put a guard on our own men.

The next morning, American shells started lobbing over. It is a kind of firing 'across his bows'. The American plan was to terrify the civilians without actually destroying the town. If rubble fell across the road, it would delay the tanks, so they wanted the road clear so they just shelled over the top of it.

The civilians quickly realised that the German army had gone. From every house a white sheet of surrender was flown. We let our lads out and they lined both sides of the road.

If you can imagine a narrow village road, with the road turning sharp left at the top, this road was lined on both sides by POWs in British army uniform. Then suddenly a huge tank swept round the corner and faced down the street ready to fight its way through. All our lads got out their handkerchiefs to wave and cheer. So our valiant American allies 'fought' their way down the street through the cheering crown of POWs.

PHASE THIRTEEN

Their officer stopped and said, 'What the hell are you doing?' We explained and he said, 'Well that's fine. You take over this town because we have got to move on.'

They were on their way to Berlin. Whether that was true or not I do not know, but that is what they said. Certainly, they were going on to Magdeburg.

It was 12 April and by now we were back in what became the Russian sector. Ummendorf was later in East Germany. Theoretically, these Americans should not have been there. Eisenhower had agreed with the Russian army that this area should be the Russian sphere of influence.

Anyway, the Americans WERE here. They unloaded a lot of food and K-rations. K-rations are concentrated food. For people who have enteritis and dysentery, I cannot think of a worse food to give them. They did not have anything else and, of course, we could not resist eating it. So that was the situation.

The Americans moved off.

Thompson said, 'Let's go to the Burgermaster.' That was a sort of mayor. We said to him, 'Call in all arms, all cameras, and all things like that.' I stole one of the cameras, which I used for years afterwards. At the same time, I stole a gun. We all stole bicycles – if any German was riding along on a bike you just pushed him off it and took the bike. It was a fairly ruthless time. This WAS the front line. Apart from the task force who released us, we were surrounded by Germans. Some of them were still fighting.

I wanted some film for my camera. I cycled down the road and went into a chemist shop and said, 'I want some film.'

He said, 'We haven't got any,' so I pulled out my revolver and pointed it at his stomach and said, 'I want some film.'

I was given seven films. I rode back and fitted one in the camera and took photographs. Which is why I now have pictures of me in Ummendorf.

I had a haircut and we cleaned ourselves up and got ready to go home. But it took a long time. We were there for seven days.

One funny episode with eggs

The one thing that was good for dysentery was eggs. Before a day or so had passed we had cleaned out every egg in the whole of Ummendorf. So one of our lads decided he would go into the next village to get eggs, which was dangerous, because, as I said, there was fighting all around.

He did not care. So he got on 'his' bike and started cycling down the road towards the next village. He was in the middle of the country when suddenly stepping out from the hedge by the side of the road came a German officer.

He held up his arms and said 'Halt! Who are you?'

The British lad said, 'I have been released by the Americans.'

'Take me to the Americans' said this officer.

The British lad said to the German officer, 'Blow you mate, I want to go and get some eggs.'

So the German pulled out his revolver, pointed it at the man and said, 'Take me to the Americans.'

So moaning and sweating and cursing, this British chap turned his bike round to walk back.

'Halt,' said the German officer and whistled. He had his whole platoon hidden behind the hedge. A fully armed platoon. I saw them marching into Ummendorf fully armed with Panzerfaust, their anti-tank weapon, over their shoulders and fully armed.

Thompson quickly said, 'Hand all the arms in.' So they handed all their arms in and went into the barn that we had been using. Thompson quickly put our men on guard.

The German officer said 'Where are the Americans?'

Thompson said, 'Well they have gone on.'

The German officer was furious. Absolutely furious. By that time he was disarmed and so were his men. Which was a bit of hard luck I suppose.

The Americans eventually sent an armed task force, with lorries, to bring us back. And so we arrived at Hildesheim, to the big airport and this was an experience.

When we got there, we were greeted by an American officer who said, 'We will try and get you away in a day. You will be home very quickly. Go into the hangars and barracks and get yourselves sorted out into groups of twenty-five, which is a Dakota load. We will get you home as quickly as we can.'

Unfortunately, because British POWs were now flooding in, they sent a stupid old twit of a British colonel, an absolute idiot, a cretin, and he decided we should not fly in American planes. We should only fly in British planes

PHASE THIRTEEN

and frankly there weren't any British planes, there were only American planes.

I think we were there for about three days before a staff officer flew in. In front of us all, he tore this colonel off a strip, 'Don't you know that the Americans are our allies?' he said. I am so glad he humiliated the man because he deserved it. He was a typical narrow-minded petty-fogging bureaucrat.

The result was that next day in the evening I got on an aeroplane, a Canadian aeroplane, on my way home. Can you imagine it? HOME?

We got on the plane in tears. It took off from a still-burning Hildesheim. You could see all the flames as it took off. It flew for half an hour and landed back in Hildesheim because it had engine trouble!

And what was worse was that every plane, American and British, was then withdrawn because General Montgomery was having his last push and another three endless days had to pass before we finally got on the plane home.

Hildesheim was a Luftwaffe barracks and on the airport were some interesting planes. There was a Heinkel III, that was the bomber that bombed London. I was surprised how small it was. It was only a twin-engine plane and did not have a big bomb load. Just like a Bristol Blenheim really.

I remember clambering all over the Heinkel III and sitting in the pilot's seat and thinking, 'isn't it small?'

Another plane they had on the tarmac was a German Fokker Wolf 190. That was the dominant German fighter plane and caused great havoc with our bombers. By the side of it was an American Thunderbolt. It was extraordinary; the little FW 190 had the pilot's cockpit at eye level. The Thunderbolt was a towering giant of a plane with an enormous engine. It was a fantastic great huge thing by the side of this little tiny FW 190. It must have been physically three or four times the size. In the end it was the Thunderbolt that managed to beat the FW190.

Being an American base, there was marvellous food. The big bands played for us. It was the first time I had heard boogie woogie. What a thrill.

But, obviously, we wanted to get home, home, home, home. And to sit on that airfield day after day, after day, in our little group of twenty-five, well ...!

Sure enough, the great day arrived – 22 April 1945. It was our turn to go. There was our twenty-five and THERE was our plane!

We trooped on it. I had handed over my revolver before I went but I still had my camera. As we clambered aboard, the pilot looked around and there were some chaps, enviously, watching us clamber on board.

He said to them, 'Do you want to go home? Well get on board then.' So the result was that our Dakota had men standing in the aisle like a bus, absolutely packed to capacity. If we had crashed nobody would have known who was on board. Off we went.

When I say 'crashed', do not forget that the war was still on. This was 22 April and the war did not finish until 8 May.

We flew low over Germany through a storm, with lightning, with rain thundering down, but we could see below us a war-torn Germany, fields criss-crossed with tank tracks, rivers with all the bridges smashed, signs of war. We eventually landed in Brussels.

I had dysentery again. So when we stopped in Brussels airport to refuel, against all instructions, I said, 'I am sorry, but I will shit my pants otherwise.' I clambered out of the plane, got down on the tarmac by the side of the plane, and squirted all over the tarmac, and then clambered back on board again.

PHASE FOURTEEN

It was 22 April 1945. After five years as a POW the view of the white cliffs of Dover was overwhelming. We were over England.

Then we flew to the west of London and I saw the power station at Neasden near to where I lived. Finally, we landed at Westcott Airport.

Westcott is an airfield just a few miles north of Aylesbury. Babs, my cousin, used to sit on a hill and watch the planes landing, knowing it was the POWs who were landing.

As we got out of the aeroplane, the RAF had arranged for each man to be met by a little WRAF (the Women's Royal Air Force) all beautifully made up, charming with a big smile, all smartly dressed. The idea being that she would welcome 'her' man.

As I jumped off the plane there was this sweet little girl waiting. I said, 'Please do not touch me.' She wanted to hold my arm and I said, 'I am lousy, I am filthy. For three months we have been on the march.' Can you imagine three months on the march, 1,000 miles in three months through war-torn Germany, the stench of death in your nostrils the whole time. We stank. We were lousy, bedraggled and I said, 'Please, please don't touch me.' When we got to the hangar, they had got a band there and they squirted DDT powder down our trousers and up our arms – which was a good thing – and they had tea and cakes. I didn't want to know, that's for sure.

Then we got in a lorry and they drove us off to Gerrards Cross.

As we drove through Aylesbury some very pleasant women stopped the lorry and said, 'If any of you have got a phone number at home, we will phone your parents and tell them you are on your way.'

I gave Dad's phone number and they phoned him straight away and said, 'We've just seen your son going through.'

I weep every time I think of that one.

But then typical of the army, I wanted to go to the lavatory again. We tried to get the driver to stop but he did not give a damn. So I made a terrible mess in my trousers. So there I was filthy, stinking and now I had shit myself, it was running down my trousers and my leg.

When we finally got to Gerrards Cross and were pushed into a room which just had paillasses on the bed, I said to the sergeant, 'I have just shit myself and I am all filthy. Can I please have a bath?'

'You get a bath tomorrow morning,' he said, 'and a new uniform.'

I said, 'Well what do I do now?'

He said, 'Oh you just put up with it.'

And put up with it I did.

So my first night at home, tears, filthy and stinking, but at least I was home.

The drive from Westcott Airfield to Gerrards Cross passing through an English countryside unspoilt by war. Beautiful, wonderful. The English countryside after the devastation of Germany, you cannot conceive what a difference there was.

Next morning, I had a shower, and got a brand-new uniform. Women were there saying, 'What unit are you?' They were sewing on our medal ribbons and our overseas service stripes and everything. It was a marvellous system.

Finally, we went to the officer and he gave us some money and said, 'There is some pocket money for you.' We had six weeks' leave.

He said, 'Later you will be told what to do but just go off and have a good holiday.'

A lorry took us to the station. I wanted to go back to Queen's Park Station, so I caught the train from Gerrards Cross to Marylebone. At Marylebone I phoned Dad and said 'I am home, will you meet me at Queen's Park?' It was a very emotional moment, I can assure you.

At Queen's Park Station there were Dad and Doug. I don't think they recognised me at first and I don't think I recognised them, but finally we managed to get together.

You cannot know how many times in the POW camp, I had dreamed of walking down the road to home. The police station I had served in had been destroyed by a bomb. So home we went.

PHASE FOURTEEN

There were Mum and Mabel and the next-door neighbours, I remember all these things as if they were yesterday. Sitting in the front room, them looking at me, me looking at them and looking round the room.

I remember saying 'You have not even changed the wallpaper!'

For me, my life would never ever be the same again and they were so untouched by the war that they had not even changed the wallpaper.

I agree that it was a ridiculous thing to say, because there had been a war on. Though in fact you would not have noticed it because, compared with Hildesheim, with its 83 per cent damage, that part of London had few gaps in its streets.

Mum said, 'We must go across and see Mr & Mrs Latcham.' This was a little grocer's shop over the road.

I remember saying, 'Look at all this food.'

And they said, 'What do you mean, it is all on points.'

And I said, 'I don't care, you have actually got it.'

The shops in Germany just had cardboard pictures of food in the window. They had no food. And there was this shop, stacked out with tins and salmon and everything else. It was on points, it was on ration, but it was there! They were very cross with me.

I was very, very unwell with this dysentery and debility.

I went to bed on 24 April and I stayed in bed until 8 May. which was VE Day – Victory in Europe Day, it was two days really – 8 May and 9 May. On the morning of 9 May, the phone rang. It was David Hatton. David said, 'John, his brother, and I are here. I am up from Gosport, John is down from Wolverhampton. We must see you this evening. We were up in the West End last night. We are going back up again to see the sights of London.'

So I said, 'OK, I will be there to meet you at 7 o'clock on Kensal Rise.'

Mum had previously said to me, 'We are going to have tea with Doug.' Doug, my father's brother, had married Eileen during the war and they just had a baby, Pat. So here was my first visit to see my new sister-in-law. As I strolled up the road, I said 'Oh, I am meeting David Hatton at 7 o'clock.'

'You can't,' said Mum, 'you are going to tea with Doug.'

And I said, 'Well I know I am going to tea with Doug. But I do not want to be there all evening.'

'Oh, Vic, you can't go.'

'I can, and I will,' I said.

They thought I was a little bit touched. I reckon they were probably right.

Anyway, I went to tea with Doug and Eileen and met Pat.

Then I said, 'Well thank you ever so much,' and went off.

On the Rise there was David Hatton with Joan his girlfriend, whom he subsequently married. And there was John Hatton with his sister Dorothy and Dorothy had her friend who was on leave from the ATS – Gertie Hayes. We went up to town. We were part of the thousands of people in Whitehall, watching Mr Churchill making his famous salute.

Little Gertie Hayes was too tiny to be able to see anything. So great big Vic Markham lifted her up. We saw the king and queen at Buckingham Palace and again I lifted her up. When we got on the tube, it was packed solid, and little Gertie Hayes sat on my knee. When we finally got home, we walked up Kensal Rise to Whitmore Gardens.

She said, 'I live down there.'

So I said, 'See you home.'

And as we were walking down the road I said, 'Look, this Gertie bit. Haven't you got a better name?'

She said, 'Well my friends call me Trudy.'

'Trudy it is then,' I said.

That was 9 May and we were married on 16 July. Best day's work I ever did. For both of us could now look forward and not have to look back.

We celebrated our Golden Wedding in 1995. We have three wonderful children and eight fantastic grandchildren.

It was all of fifteen years before I could actually bring myself to talk openly about POW life.

LETTERS HOME

We were allowed to write one letter a week home. I wrote to Dad. He wrote to me. He passed my letters on to our local paper who published some extracts. Here they are:

Kensal Rise Rover – A Prisoner of War

Mr & Mrs Reginald Markham of 4 Peploe Road, Kensal Rise, have heard this week that their son, Gunner Victor Markham of the Royal Artillery, is a prisoner of war in Germany. He was officially reported as missing in May.

Gunner Markham, a member of the 28th Willesden Rover Scouts, was called up for service last October. He went to France in March with his regiment. His letters to his parents and friends were always cheerful and in the last letter his parents received from him, dated 16 May, he said that it was getting 'noisy at nights'. No more was heard from him after that and eventually he was reported as 'missing'.

From information Mr & Mrs Markham have received, it appears that Gunner Markham's regiment was ordered to assist in holding up the German advance to enable the Dunkirk evacuation to be carried out.

On 28 May his unit was at Cassells and early that morning the only bridge over the canal was blown up, thus cutting off their retreat.

Friends will congratulate Gunner Markham on his escape and wish him a speedy return home.

Life of a War Prisoner

What is life like as a prisoner of war (POW) in Hitler's Germany? Dull, monotonous and intensely boring? It must be all that and much more, but being granted the privilege the other day of looking through a batch of letters from a captured Kensal Rise soldier, I realised what a priceless gift is that peculiarly British trait of 'making the best of things, no matter what the circumstances'.

Captured just before the Dunkirk evacuation last spring, this lad, like all other war prisoners, is allowed to write two letters and three postcards a month. From these, one can piece together a fair picture of the daily round in a German POW camp.

Those little luxuries

This Kensal rise soldier is in a camp at Thorn, in East Prussia, and his first letter home, dated last June (it arrived in November), told his parents that he was being 'treated very well'. The food, he said, was quite good, but he asked for chocolates, sweets, nuts, biscuits and Oxo.

In all his letters since, the need for such little luxuries has been emphasised.

A July letter said that gym was a morning feature at the camp, while much of their time was spent playing cards, draughts and in sing-songs.

In his August letter, the soldier described how he was captured after his unit had been surrounded for three days. He arrived in Germany, he said, on 10 June and had been made medical orderly at the camp.

Making games

His first October letter told how he was settling down, and added that he and his fellow prisoners had just received their first share in a Red Cross parcel and that he was eagerly awaiting a letter from his parents – they had already written several times.

Another letter dated in October described how they had formed a darts league at the camp and had also organised a mouth-organ band, while the medical officer was teaching them bridge. He, himself, was making monopoly and chess sets. A personal item was that he had lost ten inches round the waist whilst in captivity.

In November he reported receiving another share in a Red Cross parcel and also described a visit to a German dentist.

LETTERS HOME

Letter from home

His first December letter said how overjoyed he was to get a letter from his parents. None of the parcels they had sent to him had arrived. He had been issued with a new pair of British battledress trousers. Social events, concerts and debates were popular features at the camp, which possessed a good recreation room complete with library and stage.

In a letter dated 20 December, he reported the arrival of a parcel. 'Are we pleased?' was his comment.

In January he said he was now getting letters regularly. Reading was one of his chief occupations and he had read a book a day for the last forty days. Another interesting piece of information was that they had a camp newspaper called 'The Camp' which gave news from home.

In his letters since Christmas this captive British soldier had told how at Christmas they were given a concert by a swing band, all composed of captive professional bandsmen.

What they eat

Describing the food, he says they get a bowl of thick soup consisting of potatoes, carrots, turnips, swedes and soup powders for dinner. Once a week they have fish with the soup and on Sundays, they get a meat rissole. For tea they get one-fifth of a loaf with fat or cheese or sausage or jam. A bar of soap is issued once a month and they get plenty of razor blades.

They are housed in wooden huts with large stone oven fires and they sleep on paillasses in three-tier bunks.

It's obviously not an exciting life and let us hope that the time is not far distant when he will be set free.

Waiting for Parcels

The father of a Willesden young man who was among the British soldiers whose duty it was to hold up the German advance a year ago so that the bulk of the British Expeditionary Force (BEF) could be evacuated from Dunkirk, has asked me to make known the facts – as revealed in his son's letters – about the parcels from the Red Cross reaching prisoners of war in Germany.

We have been told, says the father, that parcels have been sent to the camps in such large numbers that not only have surplus dumps of reserves been formed but that each prisoner is receiving a parcel of food each week.

His son's letters reveal that by 10 October last he had received a quarter share in one parcel. The parcels were then arriving once a month. His next share came on 11 November. By 13 December he had received the equivalent of one whole parcel. On 20 December he had a whole parcel to himself.

First news of home

On 28 February his father's first letter dated 16 August, arrived. That was the first news of home he had had since April 1939. He had had another share in a parcel on 25 February. March 10 brought the Red Cross Christmas parcel and on the same date, on a postcard home, he wrote, 'If you folks at home could only realist how much we appreciate the Red Cross parcels, you would move heaven and earth to speed up delivery. It makes an extra meal a day and fills up the twenty hours gap we have between meals.'

And the meals – 'a bowl of thick soup consisting of potatoes, carrots, turnips, swedes and soup powder'.

'One day a week we have fish in the soup and on another day – Sunday as a rule – we receive a meat rissole with the dinner. For tea we receive one-fifth of a loaf and fat and cheese or sausage and jam. Twice a week we get a quarter of a loaf.'

What is the cause of the discrepancy between the statements issued by the Red Cross and those in this young soldier's letters? Are the Nazis deceiving the Red Cross?

A 'Gang Show' in Stalag XX-A – Written by Kensal Rise Scouter

A Kensal Rise POW, Gunner V.W.R. Markham, son of Mr & Mrs Reginald Markham of 4 Peploe Road, wrote and produced a musical comedy put on recently at a POW camp in Germany. Gunner Markham was captured in the Dunkirk retreat and is now at Stalag XX-A.

Formerly a well-known Scouter in the 28th Willesden (Kensal Rise) Scout Group, famed before the war for their stage productions, Gunner

Markham called his show 'Gangway'. It was in the real Ralph Reader tradition with a London background.

Gunner Markham wrote the songs, produced, arranged for a special orchestra and to cap it all, played the part of the villain, himself. The show, says Markham in a letter to his parents, had a terrific reception. Altogether it was staged three times and most of the camp must have seen it more than once for the theatre at Stalag XX-A holds almost everyone there, at one sitting.

Apparently, the scenery was particularly effective. It was painted by a soldier whose job in civilian life was painting scenery.

Fortnightly shows

Amateur theatricals serve to pass many otherwise weary hours in these prison camps. Gunner Markham tells his parents that they have a show every fortnight and that rehearsals are held every night. 'The fellows,' he says, 'are as keen as mustard. The stage itself is first class, with footlights and coloured lighting.'

Another recent attraction at this camp was a dance-band competition. Many of the numbers played were written by British prisoners.

Gunner Markham, his friends will be glad to know, is keeping very fit in spite of the hardships of prison camp life.

That the spirit of the prisoners is very high is illustrated by this extract from one of his letters – 'We have plenty of fun, all boys together.'

For food, they live chiefly on Red Cross parcels, and the arrival of these is always a great occasion in the camp.

Jam sessions in prison camp – our men in Poland staged Pantomime

A 'jam session' in which six bands composed of POWs in the German prison camp Stalag XX-A in Poland took part, is described by Gunner Victor Markham in a letter home to his father, who lives in Peploe Road, Kensal Rise.

Gunner Markham, who was an advertising clerk before he joined the army, says that many of the numbers played were written by the POW bandsmen, most of whom were professional dance-band musicians before the war. He manages the camp's dramatic society, which, in addition to musical comedies and plays, has staged a pantomime.

A professional scene painter provides their scenery from oddments picked up about the camp and others have provided the stage with concealed lighting.

Sunday Shows

'We have rehearsals every night and a new show every fortnight,' he writes. 'Our pantomime was *Aladdin* with a *Mikado* background. We put on two performances on Sunday.'

He also mentions the camp cinema at which films shown include *White Horse Inn* and *Jamaica Inn*.